Modest
in the
West

Modest
in the
West

An Untainted Journey of Wearing Hijab

Hadiatou Wann

Modest in the West: An Untainted Journey of
Wearing Hijab by Hadiatou Wann
Published by Hadiatou Wann
www.hadiatouwann.com

Cover photograph by Beth Brown
Cover design by Sam Smith
Copy editing by Marni MacRae
Interior design & formatted by Aeysha Mahmood

ISBN: 979-8-9873590-0-6 (print)
ISBN: 979-8-9873590-1-3 (ebook)

TABLE OF CONTENTS

Acknowledgments

I am grateful to Allah Subhanahu wa Ta'ala (the most glorified, the highest) for giving me the courage to wear the hijab and making it possible for me to share my story. A sincere appreciation to my family for loving me despite not understanding my journey; the world may know me for my work, but they have known me since I was little. And to you reading this, if you've ever complimented my hijab, thank you!

To those who helped bring my vision to life...

My photographer, Beth Brown, for capturing a breathtaking shot of my cover photo despite it being so windy that day.

My copy editor, Marni MacRae, for doing an incredible job of polishing my work without ignoring my voice and writing style.

Aeysha Mahmood, for formatting and doing the interior design of the book.

Sam Smith, for the front and back cover typography and layout.

CHAPTER 1

What is A Muslim?

For two decades, my connection to Allah Subhanahu wa Ta'ala was feeble. I used to be what you call a Muslim by mouth. I went to places where I shouldn't have been, cut my fast halfway during the Holy Month of Ramadan or sometimes didn't fast at all, didn't fulfill the five daily prayers, or open the Qur'an to learn what Allah Subhanahu wa Ta'ala expected of me. Yet when people asked me what religion I followed, I told them Islam.

I did not always dress or behave modestly as a young woman, and having boundaries was foreign to me. I was living my terrible twos in my teens, hoping that if I wasn't harming others, I was still good.

But my carelessness and lack of interest in my religion was hindering my relationship with God. I was so deeply entrenched in the worldly life that I neglected preparation for the Hereafter. I thought I knew it all, but I was adrift spiritually.

Amid being lost in a spiritual maze, I was the life of the party. The center of attention. The entertainer. The girl who had mastered Beyoncé, Ciara, Jennifer Lopez, and Usher-inspired moves and looked for every opportunity to show my skills off. If Beyoncé rolled off her back and landed on her knees to belly dance, I found a way to replicate that scene. If a party was stale and I showed up, it turned up a notch.

Being in the spotlight took me to cloud nine and made me fantasize about being a celebrity. And since I didn't make it to Hollywood, I brought Hollywood to my school. During talent shows at Manhattan International High School, I was always thrilled to orchestrate dance routines.

I got a taste of stardom when I stood in front of a three hundred-plus crowd, moving my body in ways that made me gain praise and the attention of the lustful male gaze. As I gained some popularity in high school, non-Muslims viewed me as audacious and talented, while some Muslims found me to be too much.

***

I was born in Guinea, Conakry—a former French colony situated in West Africa. Nine years of my childhood were spent in my native country before moving to the United States and continuing fifth grade. Although Guinea is a predominantly Muslim country, it was rapidly getting sucked into Western influence from when I was growing up.

My first introduction to Beyoncé was as a child, sitting in my Livingroom in Conakry. When I looked up at the Television screen and saw her dancing in a crop top, I recall admiring how flawless her skin was and how care-free she appeared.

While living in tropical Guinea, the town I grew up in for most of the year was enveloped in shocking heat waves and a brazen sun that turned a fair-skinned person shades darker. During the rainy season, the streets were flooded, and the slimy red soil stained our shoes and clothes. Even after several washes the stain barely faded.

Here and there, I spotted girls and women who wore the hijab, comfortably walking the streets of Conakry, and I didn't think too much of it. In between playing outdoor games and strolling the neighborhood with my cousin and friends, I never sought to find out why they wore the hijab, though I had an understanding that the ninjas/niqabis and hijabis were seen as pious, while the immodest women who did not wear the hijab were considered promiscuous.

***

From the age of nine, I lived in New York—the city that never sleeps. While in my Bronx middle school P.S. 212, I was not amongst the popular cliques. Nicknaming myself Lil' Fresh and joining the cheerleading squad was the closest I got to being cool.

I recall shaving my legs for the first time after seeing how flawlessly the popular Latinas in middle school looked in their capris and shorts. In our Bronx cubicle one evening, my older sister found me in the bathroom with a razor. "You know, if you start shaving your legs, they'll get hairy, right?" she asked, attempting to stop me from making an irreversible decision.

But I didn't care. I wanted to show off my legs. I wanted to fit in. As soon as my sister stepped out of the bathroom, I closed the door, stretched my legs in the bathtub, and ran the razor over the hair follicles that barely stuck out of my epidermis.

Winter in America was less nerve wracking, it meant I could cover up from head to toe and not feel different, while summertime was usually an awkward season for me. Summertime meant that girls would compete for the boldest outfit and hairstyle to get attention from the opposite gender.

I was stuck between two worlds in summer. I didn't cover from head to toe, nor was I half-naked. This was a time when girls wore crop tops and shorts; booty cheeks hanging, cleavage peek-a-booing. I was the odd one. When I kept my legs concealed in long skinny jeans even in ninety- or one-hundred-degree Fahrenheit weather, my non-Muslim friends would always ask, "Why don't you show your legs?"

In New York City, women with all types of beauty and curves roamed the streets. Whenever a curvy woman walked past a group of men, their necks elongated, jaws dropped, and eyes zoomed in on the woman's backside. "Daggg!!! Shawty packin'. Lemme holla at you for a second, ma. Lemme getcho digits, beautiful," I would hear them holler as they rushed toward the curvy woman. The girl with the biggest booty always had the spotlight, while less-curvy girls were on stand-by. These men could be found posted on the corner of the street the entire day, looking at any woman that walked by to see if she had a flatty or fatty.

Subconsciously, I began to think that wearing tight clothes that revealed every part of a woman's intimate parts was the standard of sexy. As my body developed, I too found myself in Fordham Plaza shopping around for the tightest fit. And soon, I was on the phone walking toward my house and a man hollered, "Hey, beautiful! My number is..." I looked over at him, chuckled and kept walking. It was nice being noticed, but I knew full well I would never register his number in my phone.

When Mama, me, and my siblings moved to New York, Papa stayed behind in Guinea. Papa was not home year-round in New York, but my eldest brother (who has my father's aura) was for a few years. Inside the house, I maintained some level of modesty. I couldn't walk around the house in booty shorts because my oldest brother would tell me to cover up a little. Though we were family, I grew up not wearing clothes that were too revealing around my brothers. My eldest brother, just like Papa, always encouraged me to ditch extensions and embrace my natural hair. But I was not ready to embrace my truth yet. The West had slid its grasp around me.

***

What is a Muslim? Islamic scholars describe a Muslim as someone who submits to God's will, and in turn achieves contentment. Allah Subhanahu wa Ta'ala has given me free will. Every choice or action I take either brings me closer to my Creator or diverts me from Him.

As a Muslim, I must be cautious about how my actions may affect others. If "living my best life" means harming myself and others along the way, there needs to be some adjustments. As a Muslim, I must always keep in mind that God made my body, and He has laid down rules for me to cherish and protect it as much as possible.

That means that I cannot wake up one morning and decide to get a permanent tattoo because I'm feeling adventurous or artsy. I cannot allow all men to have access to my body because I find them cute. I cannot undress myself and stand nude in the middle of Times Square because I find myself stranded in a game of Truth or Dare.

As a Muslim, I must learn to be disciplined and balanced in every area of my life. Though I identified as an African, living in a non-Muslim country in the West for the majority of my life, I found my Muslim identity slowly being neglected. The idea that I needed to sacrifice my old ways and submit to how Allah Subhanahu wa Ta'ala wants me to look and behave felt like a mountain climb.

CHAPTER 2
Doubts About Islam

I grew up in a household that was mainly focused on secular education. Back in Guinea, my father worked from sunrise to past dusk as director of a printing press so my siblings and me could attend private schools and for food to always be present on the table.

Most mornings, while birds sung, chirped, and flew from one coconut tree to the next and medium-sized lizards crawled the cemented floor, for our morning routine my father seated my siblings and me around a white oval table on the terrace. Papa gave us a glass of milk, honey, and fromage and posed general culture questions to ensure we knew what was going on in the world.

When Papa had some free time, he would take my siblings and me to the library. He expected me to get good grades, hang around the right crowd, and maintain a natural look (i.e., no extensions in my hair and no miniskirts or shorts).

One afternoon, when I was around eight years old, for the first time I decided to let someone put extensions in my hair because I saw other girls and women gracefully wear them. I, too, wanted longer hair. Upon my father's return from work, he took a pair of scissors, grabbed me, and cut off the extensions. My eyes filled with tears, but I was still daddy's girl.

Although my mother had an engineering degree, she took time off to be a stay-at-home mom. When she wasn't helping us with our homework, looking for outfits to adorn my siblings and me, cleaning up our boogers, or chasing after us, she would dye garments, tablecloths, and bedsheets, selling them to locals and office workers. She would often travel to Dakar to buy merchandise, reselling the items upon returning to Conakry. With my mother, I could easily get away with sliding a few extensions in my hair. Mama couldn't resist when I gave her the puppy eyes.

The only memories I had of my forefathers were a few paintings or black and white photos and stories my parents told me of them. My paternal grandfather was strict and highly respected; a successful businessman and Qur'an teacher who in his lifetime had taught the word of Allah Subhanahu wa Ta'ala to over four thousand students.

Throughout my childhood, I would also be reminded of my paternal great grandfather three generations down who left Fouta Toro (in Senegal) and settled in Fouta Djallon (in Guinea) in 1812 and was amongst the leaders who spread Islam.

It was moving to learn about my forefathers' character and impact, but it also meant that I had to limbo my way to meet the high expectations that were set. Whenever I or anyone in my family did anything that was non-Islamic, people would say, "the grandchild of ____ did such and such." There was a double standard. No room for error. Our actions—good or bad—were always compared to those of my forefathers.

***

During my visit to my native country in 2013, Papa and I stopped by to greet a friend of his. On our way to leave, his friend—whom I had never met prior to that trip—handed me a translated copy of the Qur'an in French.

When I returned to the United States, I put the Qur'an away and didn't bother to read it. Up to that point, I wasn't habitual in praying the five obligatory daily prayers, nor was I familiar with the teachings of the Qur'an. Still, I considered myself Muslim. Looking back now, I realized that the gift (the Qur'an) was Allah Subhanahu wa Ta'ala calling me toward Him, but I missed His call because I was distracted.

Even as a young girl, I remember always looking up at the sky and being conscious that there was a higher power. I was told that the higher power was called Allah and I was Muslim. But I didn't know why?

The part about Islam I had a hard time accepting was polygamy. In my community, when I saw or heard stories of people who practiced Polygamy, I was disturbed. I could not grapple with the idea of several women sharing a man, and the heartache and headache that could come with it. In my mind, Muslim men had the power to wake up one morning and marry another woman without discussing with his previous wife or wives. As a woman, it made me feel like I was powerless. And that did not sit well with me.

As far as I was concerned, Islam was a religion that favored men and gave them the power to do as they wished. A cloud of doubts began to form inside me about Islam, and I didn't bother to learn more about the religion. My mind was sealed, and there wasn't an explanation out there that could make me see things differently.

CHAPTER 3

Deciding to Wear the Hijab

In America, I attended schools where most students, staff, and faculty were non-Muslims. Outwardly, nothing indicated my Islamic identity. When I told them that I was Muslim, they would respond in shock, "You're Muslim?"

As a non-hijabi observing from a distance, I thought that hijabis were too hard on themselves and people-phobic. On summer days they were always wrapped up in layers of clothes even though they were noticeably brewing in them, they stayed isolated from men, and rarely socialized. I thought, *That could never be me.*

One summer afternoon, as newlyweds, my husband at the time and I visited his mother. I wasn't committed to hijab then. That day, I wore a tight, long-sleeve shirt that reached slightly below my waist and tight jeans that hugged my curves. My mother-in-law at the time—who just came from Hajj (the religious pilgrimage Muslims must fulfill at least once in their lives if they are physically and financially able to)—calmy hinted that now that I was married, I needed to cover a little more. I could tell that deep down she wished I wore the hijab. But in the back of my mind, I told myself, 'Once I reach old age.'

About a year prior to deciding to wear the hijab, I had a dream. The dream was short and blurry, but I saw a woman with a black hijab on. I remember waking up and thinking, *There's no way I could wear the hijab now.* It was too soon.

That would mean forever giving up on wearing the thing that boosted my confidence and gave me an exotic look—extensions. It meant being held to a high standard; if I make a mistake, it would be aggrandized. The love of God was in my heart, but I was not prepared to adjust my ways to level up to Allah's standard for me.

By then, I had already begun listening to Islamic lectures from my favorite religious leader, which were meaningful and easy to understand. On different occasions when I listened to them, I would hear the reminder, "My sister, cover your hair." But the message did not seep into my heart at that moment.

Then, I started seeing hijabis frequently when I went out. When I looked at them, there was a void in me. I felt I was not doing what I was supposed to do as a Muslimah. *It must be easy for them. Or they must have grown up used to the hijab lifestyle,* I thought to myself as I compared myself to hijab-wearing women and piled up more excuses not to wear the veil.

I told myself that when I reached old age and went to Hajj that I would put on the hijab, but until then, the minimum I was going to do was refrain from putting extensions in my hair.

But my conscience shook me. I began thinking *What if I die before old age? Allah*

Subhanahu wa Ta'ala could tell me that He sent me several signs so that I could wake up and become a better practicing Muslim. What then would I tell Allah? That I loved showing off my body and hairstyles more than obeying his command?

Shortly after ending my atrocious marriage, I traveled to another country to be around family. The trip gave me room to refresh my mind and begin the process of healing. Up until then, I still had no intention of putting on the hijab, but I was transitioning into a lifestyle free of wigs.

For someone who was used to wearing long extensions and switching hairstyles frequently, my options were little if I stopped doing so. With my natural hair there was only so much I could do before becoming bored. I looked for reasonable excuses/benefits as motivation to put on the hijab. I convinced myself that if I chose to wear the hijab for good, at least I could wear different colors and designs.

When I returned to the states a month later, by then my heart was beginning to soften. One day, while at work and listening to a lecture by one of my favorite leaders, I realized that I had been ungrateful to Allah Subhanahu wa Ta'ala.

I got up from the styling chair, went into the bathroom, and looked at myself in the mirror.

It's time to put on the hijab, I promised myself.

With the many Muslims around the world striving to engage in acts that please Allah Subhanahu wa Ta'ala, I became concerned as I immersed myself in Islamic lectures that reminded me that if I didn't try to do what pleased my Creator (i.e., wearing the hijab), He would replace me with others who were willing to do that which I refused to do for His sake.

Oh, this made me jealous.

The healthy type of jealousy that motivated me to better myself and join the ranks of those who strove to please Allah. I didn't want to miss out on getting extra rewards and getting closer to God, nor did I want to be replaced. I, too, wanted to gain the love of Allah.

On an October morning, I made my Niyyah (intention) to change my life, repented, and asked Allah to assist me throughout my journey as I committed to hijab. That same day, when I opened my closet, I grabbed some of the revealing outfits I commonly wore and put them in a bag to give them away. I wanted to eliminate as much temptation as possible because I didn't know if I would reach a point where I missed those clothes and go back to my old ways.

Individuals who wear the hijab are noticeable in all the spaces they occupy. As they interact with the world, they are bound to come across people who understand why they wear the hijab and those who don't. In Islam, girls are ordered by Allah Subhanahu wa Ta'ala to wear the hijab once they reach the age of puberty. The hijab is more than the covering of the head and body—it signifies the wearer's dedication to do what pleases her Creator and adhere to the Islamic way of life.

At the age of twenty-six, I put on the hijab and decided to rededicate my life to embracing an Islamic lifestyle. Had I died prior, who knows what my fate would have been in the Hereafter. Luckily, Allah Subhanahu wa Ta'ala was patient with me and gave me time to rectify myself. It didn't matter that I lagged compared to girls who wore the hijab as soon as they reached puberty, nor did I think I was better than Muslim women who were older than me but did not wear the hijab. This was my journey; it was my moment to show God how much I was willing to improve myself.

When I began wearing the hijab and posted my very first photo on social media, it was like the world stopped for a moment. At least in my social media space. Although my decision seemed sudden to people, behind the scenes I was taking baby steps to prepare myself for the leap of a lifetime.

Even though I didn't intend for my decision to cover to affect others, I experienced different types of reactions from Muslims and non-Muslims. There were people who drew closer to me, and others who distanced themselves from me. Some were reluctant to approach me, as if suddenly I put on a spooky mask. *Hello, relax, it's me, Hadiatou. Don't be afraid. I'm still the same person, just more modest.*

My commitment to wearing hijab came three months after I ended my first marriage—an ordeal only Allah Subhanahu wa Ta'ala could have gotten me out of. When I was at my lowest, my Creator was there to protect me. I was beyond grateful that Allah safely helped to end a marriage that was harrowing, and decided what better way to show my Lord my appreciation than to do an act He loves.

When I began wearing the hijab, people who thought I was still married could have assumed that I wore the hijab because of my husband. Others who knew I had gotten divorced could have assumed that I wore it to improve my image from the stigma of divorce. From the outside looking in, whether they knew I divorced or not, many had assumptions of why I went from not wearing the hijab to wearing it full-time. However, I had my own reasons. Though people may have assumed that I'd just woken up overnight and put on the hijab, I was in fact going through an internal jihad for two years before I decided to fully embrace the hijab. First, I stopped braiding my hair with extensions, then, slowly, I decided to wear wigs instead of weaves. This permitted me to corn row my hair without extensions. It meant that when it was time to pray, within seconds I could remove my wig, fulfill prayer, and once I finished worship, throw back on my neat-looking wig and step out into the world. I became comfortable with this strategy, and, in fact, I was planning on doing this until I reached old age.

My decision to wear the hijab was a bitter pill my parents had to swallow. Their entire lives revolved around protecting me like an egg. With this change, they knew that they were not in control. They feared the mistreatment I could potentially face in an anti-Muslim society.

I'll never forget the worried look I saw on my father's face when he visited us in New York in 2020. On our way to the neighborhood mosque, as I walked beside him, he commented on the black jilbab I wore. "Avoid wearing dark colors, it's not safe for you here," Papa said in French.

Since high school, long before I even put on the hijab, I had developed a love for the color black. Black made me feel beautiful and bold. But all of a sudden, Papa wanted me to stop wearing black and walk on egg-shells? Kim Kardashian could show up to the Met Gala in a face-covering and head-to-toe black bodysuit and be called a fashionista. But when I wore my black jilbab in my neighborhood, I'd be seen as a threat? You could talk me out of eating salad, but you could not convince me to stop wearing black.

In 2021, my cousin, who lived in Austria and ran a blog, invited me as a guest on her Facebook live to discuss my book projects. As I was interviewed, she was startled to see my transition into a hijab-wearing woman. "How are you able to wear the hijab in New York City?" she asked in my native language and in front of her virtual audience toward the end of the live.

That question made me ponder for a moment. I had gotten so comfortable wearing the veil by then that I was almost oblivious to the fact that I lived in one of the largest cities in the world, where maintaining the hijab was a great challenge due to the rise of Islamophobia. However, my acceptance of the hijab did not occur overnight. It had been quite a journey.

Putting on the hijab had a Domino Effect on every aspect of my life. The new version of me retired from needing to suck up all the attention in a room. I am now completely comfortable with being in the shadows and letting others be in the spotlight.

Growing up exposed to pop culture, when celebrities like Usher, Trey Songz, and Chris Brown lifted their shirts, girls and women—including myself—melted. It was normal for me to stare as much as I wanted when the opposite gender was attractive and flexed his muscles or abs.

But when I started wearing hijab, Allah Subhanahu wa Ta'ala put hyaa (shyness) over my eyes. Now, I feel uncomfortable looking at the opposite gender for too long. And if he shows off the parts of him that are enticing, I instantly look away. And if by looking at the same or opposite gender for too long evokes jealousy and/or envy in me, I quickly look away so that it doesn't affect my heart.

I also became wary about places I frequented, what I looked at, and what traveled through my ears. I invested most of my time watching and listening to content that educated me (whether it was related to secular or religion) and boosted my spirituality. When I did follow a select few influencers, I made sure that their content would not eat away at what I was aiming for spiritually. Leaning in to accepting prohibitions in Islam and applying them in my life didn't mean that I had to shut myself off from the world. I simply had to decipher what I was going to allow into my world to live my best Islamic life.

As soon as family and friends found out that I was back on the market after getting divorced, they asked if they could match me with someone. I wasn't ready then. I was going through the motions of putting my torn heart back into one piece and spiritual growth. But my mother worried that because I was now covered, it would be harder to attract a husband.

"Now, to find a husband, you have to go to the mosque and marry an imam," Mama said in my native language, with all seriousness.

"When the time is right, my husband is going to find me, Insha Allah (God willing)," I told her.

"How is he going to find you when you're always inside?" Mama asked.

I mean, what was I supposed to do in the middle of a pandemic? Walk around like a mailwoman, knock on people's doors, and ask them if they were looking for a wife? Alhamdulillah (all praise is due to God), when the time was right, my husband found me through recommendation. I was indoors.

When I remarried, it wasn't to an imam, but it was to a man who appreciated my modesty. I could be completely modest in public, but in our home I could unwind, wear whatever I wanted, be my husband's biggest fantasy, and be rewarded by Allah. That feeling of now having parts of me reserved and not on public display made me embrace the beauty of hijab even more.

I had been fixed in my ways, and with the amount of ego I had, no person close to me had the power to convince me to wear the hijab. Not an in-law nor society. Only Allah Subhanahu wa Ta'ala, through His wisdom, patience, and mercy, had the power to do so. I didn't wear the hijab to meet others' standards, earn respect in society, improve my image as a divorcee, nor attract a religious husband later. I decided to wear the hijab because I felt I had been ungrateful to my Creator for many years, and it was time to make it up to Him by doing what pleases Him most.

CHAPTER 4
Hijab and Business

Although I was surrounded by Muslims in Guinea, I grew up seeing complete strangers (men and women) shaking hands. I thought it was the norm. When I moved to the United States, it was similar. In school and outside of school, hugging and shaking hands with the opposite gender was just a way of saying hello. But little did I know, Islamically, I was not supposed to.

During freshman year of undergrad, I began working as a sales representative for a nutrition company. At the time, I was not wearing hijab and had entered the world of business. This role gave me the courage to stand in the bustling streets of

34th St. and 42nd St. in Times Square and step in front of any stranger to talk about the products that the company offered.

In the business world, one of the etiquettes was having a firm handshake. And we were taught that a customer's first impression of us influenced their buying decision, so we dressed to impress! When I stepped out to do business, I threw on my power suit, hopped on my high heels, grabbed my business cards and products/catalog, and aimed for a sale. In dealing with all types of customers (men and women), giving a firm handshake was a reflex.

Gender Interactions

By the time I started wearing the hijab, I was not working for the nutrition company anymore. But since I was now an author, I would still be out in the world, at times interacting with both genders, which meant that I had to adapt to the Islamic guidelines when it came to dealing with the oppositive gender.

It had not occurred to me how much other Muslims and non-Muslims were unaware of the Islamic way of interacting with the opposite gender until I took my hijab seriously. Prior to wearing the hijab, I thought that only niqabis (Muslim women who wear garments that cover their faces) refrained from shaking hands with the opposite gender. Upon gradually learning the rules of hijab, it became apparent to me that there was a double standard placed on hijabis/niqabis, although all Muslim men and women (hijabi and non-hijabi) were obliged to refrain from shaking the hands of the opposite gender who were not immediate family members.

As much as I wanted to make sure that I wasn't shaking the opposite gender's hand, I did err. In the beginning of my hijab journey, I attended an award ceremony, where a woman I knew introduced me to a respected attendee. My immediate response was to shake his hand. After doing so, I realized that I had made a mistake. The people around me didn't think too much of it because they most likely didn't know the Islamic rules of engagement with the opposite gender, but internally I quickly said Astaghfirullah (I seek forgiveness in Allah).

Being in an environment where everyone was hugging or shaking hands with the opposite gender made me feel like the odd one out. Those who didn't know why I now abstained from shaking the hands of the opposite gender may have thought that I was a germaphobe or simply stuck up. Somehow someway, I had to get used to the new version of me.

I recall my first public appearance as a hijabi. Men and women came to my book reading/signing to show support. As one Muslim male approached me for a photo, he aimed to put his arm over my shoulder. "You're not supposed to touch me," I pointed out. Instantly, he kept a reasonable distance between us, then the photo was taken. The old me wouldn't have said anything, because after all it's just a photo and I'm not going home with him, right? But Islamically, it is not allowed because prevention is better than a cure.

I still wanted to pursue my passions and be friendly, but I also had to make sure that if I was going to continue doing business, I wasn't compromising my commitment to gaining Allah's pleasure.

CHAPTER 5
The Job Search

Hair maintenance was a big deal to me even as a child. On days when my hair was neglected and I noticed that others had theirs done, I snapped into a tantrum. "Look at my hair," I would say in my native language and burst into tears as I complained to my mother. This was my way of guilt-tripping Mama into doing or paying for my hair to get braided as quickly as possible.

At the age of three, Mama told me, whenever she started unraveling her braids or my sister's, I would whip the comb out of her hands and attempt to help her even though I didn't know how to. I would do the same for my cousins and aunt. Then whenever I saw any woman, even if her hair was braided and she had no intentions of taking her braids out, I would beg her to let me do so. My mother noticed that I loved playing with hair. "This one is going to be a hairdresser," she would say in my native language.

From a tender age, I practiced braiding my dolls' hair and over the years had developed a deeper passion for doing hair. So much so that when I moved to New York, I began working at a hair salon as a teenager. I went to school on weekdays and could not wait for the weekend so I could work at the salon, which was less than a five-minute walk from my house.

I was excited about having a commission-based income and was thrilled at how I was able to make people feel through hair braiding. Given that the hairstyles clients chose sometimes took three to four hours to complete, it turned into a therapy session. We discussed different topics and personal stories were shared.

The hair salon was a client's second home, and I the hair braider was their beauty doctor and confidant. They walked into the hair salon insecure about their hair and walked out confident and rejuvenated. When I was assigned to service a client of a different race than me, discrimination/racism disappeared into the deep basin sink as I washed their hair. Because at that moment, they trusted me to take care of what made them feel most attractive. Their hair.

***

Six months into my transition as a hijabi, I was still working as a hair braider, providing services to children, women, and men of different races. My specialty was any design of cornrows, box braids, knotless/feed-in braids, jumbo and micro braids, crochet braids, tracks, full weave, and wig installation/lace fronts. I had been working in the hair industry for a decade and aspired to open my own salon.

While working in two African hair braiding salons in a decade, unintentionally I became a go-to hairdresser. Children that were hard to control/manage and were tender headed calmed down as soon as I began braiding their hair. Women who were labeled difficult clients and didn't tip other braiders tipped me when I finished styling their hair. As for the men, whether it was attraction or my service, they always requested me. When a client requested a specific hair braider, the request had to be met.

As a New Yorker, I've had the opportunity to be surrounded by all types of cultures and faith, but the Orthodox Jews stand out to me for one reason—they aren't afraid to look Jewish even through changing times. Orthodox Jewish men are always seen clothed in a black suit, a Shtreimel fur hat or Fedora, and two strands of long hair hanging by their ears. This look differentiates them from others. They are intentional about it even if they are discriminated against.

It was a slow day at the salon, which meant I had the chance to relax before the next walk-in. The Eyewitness News came on the screen, and I could not believe what my eyes saw. But then again, it happened in New York—where all bizarre things take place.

As seen on Eyewitness News, an Orthodox Jew was walking and suddenly, a male walked up to him and slapped his hat off. Without creating a scene, the Orthodox Jew put his hat back in its place and kept walking. He had been a victim of Anti-Semitism in broad daylight. Though I was nowhere near him, I felt his pain. I imagined the times hijab wearing women were victims of religious discrimination.

Although Orthodox Jews are not accepted in some places, they are adamant about following their teachings. This is a constant reminder to me that in a world where there is a rise in Islamophobia, even if my hijab makes others poke fun at me or label me harshly, I am to keep walking and remain firm upon my religious stance.

Braiding hair was not only soothing to me, but it also gave me the opportunity to exert my artistic side and provided a flexible schedule that allowed me to go to school and be an author on the side. Initially, once I began wearing hijab, my plan was to wear the hijab and work there until I secured a job in corporate America. However, with the hijab on, I slowly began to feel uncomfortable touching hair extensions and men who were not my immediate family.

Having listened to a slew of Islamic lectures and being armed with more knowledge, not applying what I learnt would have been irresponsible. Knowing that a sin is multiplied when one promotes it, I felt I was being hypocritical. If I was putting hair extensions in my hair alone, the sin would have fallen only on me. But it wasn't the case. I put extensions in the hair of several clients.

As a new hijabi, I was in a position where I stopped putting extensions in my hair, but I was still putting it in clients' hair. This meant that I was still at the forefront of promoting something that was Islamically forbidden. My conscience told me I had to put a stop to it. I had to tame my emotional attachment to extensions and wave goodbye to lulling men to sleep with my touch and getting tipped for it.

I confided in my boss, who had become like an aunt to me, about my decision. First, I stopped taking male clients. Then I decided I shouldn't even put extensions in other women/children's hair. Shortly after, I decided I shouldn't be working in an environment that promoted what was Islamically forbidden. So, I detached myself from my comfort zone and left.

It was a tough decision to make. I didn't have another job ready for me when I quit. Some of my family members told me that it wasn't a smart move and that I should never leave a job without first having a replacement. But I just couldn't be there anymore. My commute to work was short, my boss was the sweetest, and my co-workers were like family, but I wanted Barakah (blessings) in my income.

When I left, the owner of the salon would inform me that my clients were still asking to schedule an appointment with me. I felt guilty that I couldn't be there to cater to them, but I had to stick with my decision.

I never said goodbye to my clients. The last time I braided hair with extensions, I was concerned that if I told my clients that I would no longer do their hair, they might never walk in that salon again. It was my personal journey to pleasing God, but I didn't want my absence to cause the salon's profit to drop.

I left it to the owner to break the news to them that I had quit. But I believe it was also a heavy burden for the owner to carry. When customers called in to book me, she told them that I wasn't around. As the seasons changed, common sense eventually told them that I had quit. Most of my clients were non-Muslim, so they could not understand. To them, it was just horsehair, and I wasn't harming clients. But to me, I was harming my spirituality. I wasn't walking away from my dream; I was walking away from extensions. For good.

Although I didn't know that I would wear the hijab in my twenties, due to my life experiences and background education I was always certain that I would pursue business for the rest of my life. Since hijab was going to remain, my business goals also remained. All I needed to do was merge the two to live my life, complementing Islamic ethics and my standards.

As I searched for a job, I had an idea of opening a hair salon for women and girls that would promote braiding hair without extensions. This would be a great way to help them embrace their natural hair. Just because I stopped working at a hair salon didn't mean that my dream/passion for helping people feel and look beautiful died. I figured if no one was going to hire me, I was better off starting my own business, and Mama agreed to help.

Renting commercial space in New York would have been the quickest way to grow gray hair and make my wallet wail. So, I began searching for commercial space in a state nearby. After browsing the net, I found a twelve-hundred-square-foot space in Philadelphia for $1,600 per month, plus some fees. The price was perfect compared to New York listings.

I planned out how I was going to leverage my time. Only a one-hour-and-seventeen-minute drive from my house, I was prepared to have a corporate job (when I found one), hire commission-based hairdressers, and position my mother as the manager while I handled the marketing and made frequent trips to the salon to ensure business was operating smoothly.

I was able to speak directly to the owner over the phone, who was Caucasian. He knew I was Black. Through his reassurance that he did not discriminate, I felt I had found the right person to rent from. I thought, *Great, here's a Caucasian who's not racist and is willing to entrust me with his estate.* I explained my intentions, and he was delighted and even proposed having his son help with marketing if I needed services. The photos and description displayed online caught my attention, but I needed to see the space in person before signing a contract.

A few weeks after the initial call with the owner, my mother and I drove to Philadelphia to examine the location. The commercial space was close to stores, restaurants, and the road. The walls were freshly painted white, and the floor tiles were being renovated. The natural light from outside permeated the windows and unified with the indoor artificial lights, which gave the room a bright aesthetic.

I was awed at how spacious the place was compared to the asking price. *Why has no one rented this place yet?* I wondered. *This is meant to be mine.* As my eyes roamed the room, I could already picture where the reception desk would be placed, the magazine/book rack, the distance between the front desk to where the styling stations and hood dryers would be situated, and how high the mirrors were going to be hung on the walls. *This is it!* I thought. *This is the type of salon space I always imagined having.*

After showing us around, we stood there, impressed, as the owner briefly talked about his family. He mentioned that he had a family member who was racist but that he wasn't. The entire time he spoke he stared at my hijab.

After that initial in-person meeting, communication was cut off. Whether it was his concern or someone who advised him, I knew that the reason was my hijab. I reminded myself that I didn't want to be where I wasn't welcome anyway, and when I sat down at home and gathered my thoughts, I remembered that there was a beer, vape, and cigar (which Muslims are advised to stay far away from) shop in the vicinity of the commercial space. Was I so focused on securing a business location that I ignored the surrounding businesses?

Although I was disappointed that the owner was turned off by my hijab, I told myself that Allah knows what's best for me and He was protecting me and my potential business. I convinced myself that it wasn't the right time and place to open a salon. My job search continued.

I spent many months looking for a job, applying to all types of office/corporate jobs where I thought my background education would make it easy for me to get hired. As a Black woman wearing the hijab, the stakes were now higher. My photo on LinkedIn showed that I was a Muslim. Nothing screams louder 'we don't want you here' than going on an employer's Meet Our People/Staff page and seeing that not one person looked like me.

When I did come across a Black woman in the Meet our Staff section, I subconsciously scrolled down to see if I could also spot at least one Black woman who wore the hijab. I would get to the bottom of the page and still not one Black woman who wore the hijab was to be found. Given the long history of segregation in the United States, what this said to me is that they had a hard time accepting Black people, but they would rather have amongst them a Black person who was not a Muslim.

Some of my family members went as far as to say that I would never secure a good job or thrive in my carrier as an author with the hijab on. I was told to put another photo of myself on LinkedIn where I did not have my hijab on until I secured a job. And when I did secure a job to throw on a hat and not wear the full hijab, which covered my neck.

As absurd as this sounded to me, they were serious about it. But I was even more serious about my dedication to keep my hijab on. Wearing the hijab while living in the United States required me to have a I don't care-what you think-about my-hijab attitude to ward off naysayers. If I didn't, the hijab would not have lasted on my head.

I kept looking, until I secured one interview. From the interviewer's voice I had the impression that I would be called for another interview. But I didn't get a second call. I had been working since I was a teenager. This was my first time being unemployed for so long.

The only hope I held onto was pondering over the verse that constantly came up in the Islamic lectures I listened to, which promised that if anyone left something for the sake of Allah, Allah would replace it with something better. I was certain that because I quit working at a salon where extensions were used, Allah would give me a better job.

I had graduated with my bachelor's and was seeking a steady source of income. My salon project was put on hold, and because I had renewed my relationship with Allah Subhanahu wa Ta'ala, I also became pickier with the type of jobs I could do. It was no longer whether I was qualified for the position, but did the job qualify according to my beliefs. I applied to several corporate jobs I deemed fit for me and was rejected.

What crossed my mind at that moment was during my teenage years I had heard stories of adults who migrated to America and tweaked their names to sound more American, lessening their chances of job rejection. But there was no way I was going to change my name just for a job. And even if I changed my name and got the job, the color of my skin and hijab would follow me to work. And who knew what kind of treatment I would get once I showed up to work with the latter.

Being discriminated against during my job search may have been the best thing for me. Maybe, just maybe, it was Allah's way of showing me that I was not being completely honest with what I wanted for myself.

Would I have sincerely looked forward to walking into an office job every day, being glued to a chair, and taking commands from rude hierarchy? Because to be honest, my ideal vision for my life was to create and run my own empire, leave my bed when I wanted, and not be glued to a chair nine-to-five. Why then did I keep applying and waiting to be picked? Was I acting out of desperation?

When I confided in one of my siblings about how hard it was finding a good-paying corporate job as a hijabi and Black woman, he advised me to accept a job offering, temporarily, even if it wasn't in the field that I studied in. Painstakingly, I took my eldest brother's advice and began applying to all kinds of jobs I thought I could handle and that met the Islamic standards.

I told myself that I would work any-where but at Amazon, given I heard stories about their enormous workload.

After circling around for nine months and going through more job rejections, where did I end up?

CHAPTER 6

Conversations with Christians

I ended up at Amazon. Working at a warehouse was the last place I wanted to be, but I believe that's exactly where God wanted me. All the rejections only to end up at a warehouse. At first, I could not understand how I was qualified for many positions but somehow ended up at a warehouse. I was frustrated, but I swallowed my pride and took the job offering. I had to trust God's wisdom.

While I was applying at Amazon, it showed that the position would be in my town. But the online application kept redirecting me to a position outside of my town. I told myself that I'd rather choose a long commute than be unemployed.

A few days before I was required to report to my first day on the job, I had to attend a self-drug testing (oral) site and mail the kit to a lab. Followed by an extensive training, which I completed on my phone in several sittings. It was the longest training I'd ever had. Amazon ensured that as a new employee I was aware of the high standards the company kept.

There was a hijabi animated character in some parts of the training. It was as if they knew I was an incoming hijabi employee and sent me a tailormade training. Out of the millions of employees Amazon hired, a hijabi was receiving a warm welcome to their workplace. It made me SMILE! *Great job, Human Resources!* I thought. Instantly, I got the impression that Amazon was trying to be inclusive.

I was fully engrossed in the Amazon brand, living the full business-customer-employee experience (i.e., I published and distributed my books through Amazon, shopped on Amazon, and worked for Amazon). Working there was going to give me an opportunity to see how the number one e-commerce company in the world operated business successfully and maintained a competitive advantage.

We (the employees) were called Amazonians, and the warehouse had been open for less than four months when I got hired. We were the first batch of employees to inaugurate it. From the day I took an employee photo for my badge to my first day at work, the people I encountered showed me a kindness I did not foresee.

Since I had never been or worked in a warehouse, I didn't know what to expect. I had thought that though Amazon's website presented everything nice and neat to appeal to customers, behind the scenes—the warehouse—would resemble a haunted house; somber, dusty boxes scattered everywhere, spiderwebs and bats hanging in the ceiling.

But the Amazon warehouse was the opposite. The floor tiles were gleaming—you could take a nap on them. Giant, new machines that each looked like it cost more than a house were aligned perfectly, and so were thousands and thousands of boxes stacked up in bins that nearly reached the ceiling. Every day, I walked into work thinking, *Jeff Bezos is not playing! This man is on a mission to take over the world.*

From the first day of work, my number one concern was how I would make sure that I fulfilled prayer on time. I spoke with some associates to let them know, and instantly I was directed to my manager. When I walked up to my manager for the first time to show my prayer schedule, he said, "I know. I'm Muslim, too." I couldn't help but smile. What a relief; someone at the warehouse could understand me.

Not only was my manager Muslim, but I was also pleased that Amazon gave an African the opportunity to rise to a managerial position. He informed me that there was a prayer room. A prayer room? I was ecstatic! Plus, it had become a standard for all Amazon warehouses to have a prayer room. Amazon won my heart with this one!

The required ten-hour shift was for the fit. One thing was clear, a couch potato could not last a day working at Amazon. With not even one chair in sight in the work area, no one sat down outside of break hours (even managers). It was set up this way to clearly communicate to us that we were not there to squander time.

While working at the Amazon warehouse I met every kind of person. The old, young, blind, deaf, and gay. A furloughed elderly English professor, architect, and a Rutgers University MBA graduate. Manpower was essential for the high demands Amazon needed fulfilled. So, if anyone passed the drug test, criminal background check, and could lift a finger, he or she got hired at the warehouse, and as each day went by, I built rapport with associates.

Outwardly I looked Muslim because I had on the hijab, so they approached me with questions about Islam. I did my best to clarify the misconceptions they had, and I also had the opportunity to ask them questions about their faith.

After a few months, my highly competitive manager was moved to the night shift, and another was assigned to us; a brolic veteran who had served in the military for seventeen years. Among the places he'd served in was Afghanistan. When he told us that he had active duty in Afghanistan—a Muslim country—my first reaction was "Uh oh."

We were on military time. If anyone came in one minute late, he or she got pulled over to the side to receive a termination warning. When he watched over us, he stood somewhere he could easily see everyone and scanned the room. His eyes were as sharp as binoculars. Every time I had to stop work tasks and walked over to the prayer room, I thought he would question me or tell me that I was taking too many breaks. He looked at me, but he never said a word.

Work began to feel more like bootcamp. It was as if somewhere in his cadet mind we were soldiers who had to climb over wooden walls to help keep his rates up and cancel other managers' scores. When he wasn't pushing us to hit quotas, he was cracking jokes and sharing military stories.

Although the first Amazon warehouse I worked for had become a place I was comfortable being in and had gotten along well with the other associates, I had to relocate because toll fees reached thousands of dollars within a few months due to my commute from where I lived to outside of town, so I decided to transfer to an Amazon warehouse in my town.

The second Amazon warehouse I was transferred to was older, much bigger, and even more fast-paced than the first. Working at Amazon opened my eyes even more to the way Muslims were viewed. My first day reporting to work, I felt like so many eyes were on me. It was as if their stares said, "oh no, a Muslim amongst us. Here comes a terrorist attack." But when moments passed and they realized that they were still alive, their faces looked relieved.

Once, as I was having lunch in the break room, there was a slim, long-haired Caucasian or Hispanic man who sat across from me. With his meal on the table and his phone in his hands, he would glare at the screen. On-and-off he stared at me and my food as if he had seen an alien having lunch in front of him. I know, I know. You're probably thinking how did I know he was looking at me if I wasn't also looking at him?

I was looking at him because I wondered if he'd ever sat that close to a Muslim, and if he thought that the food we ate was not from earth. I looked at him wishing I could at that moment have access to his thoughts. Then I looked up again and saw clutched around his neck a necklace with a cross. Suddenly, it all made sense to me. He was a Christian who was deep-rooted in his beliefs.

A few minutes flew by, and he got up and left. *Did my presence make him feel uncomfortable to the point where he could no longer bear it and left?* I queried for a second. *Oh, his break time is over.* I realized. Feeling relieved that the reason he left was because obviously he wasn't going to be paid for having lunch all day, I still thought, *What if he had questions for me about Islam?* There was a conversation that needed to be had, but I never got to find out.

For some time, I saw a dark-skinned man in the department I worked in. He resembled one of my relatives so much, but since I was now covered, I didn't think he recognized me. I wondered if my relative had ended up at the warehouse, too. He looked at me as well. But I didn't know what his reason was. On that day, almost at the end of the shift, they placed him next to my station. As I worked, I felt like the entire time he was watching me. As I waited for the pod to arrive, I picked up my phone.

"You know you're not supposed to be texting right?" he said.

I looked over at him for a second and proceeded with my task.

"Only if you're texting me," he said.

"Why would I text you when I can talk to you here?" I responded. Which was my indirect way of saying you won't get my number but the least I can do is treat you like a human being and answer you in-person.

As I continued to work, I had a feeling he was still watching me, and out of nowhere he said, "Teach me about Islam."

"What do you want to know about Islam?" I responded.

"Why are Muslims violent? I'm afraid of Muslims," he expressed. "I'm Christian," he added, and paused to look at my reaction.

I wasn't sure if he wanted me to run away from him or stop speaking to him because he said he was Christian. Appearing calm and collected, I responded, "Okay. I understand."

"Islam is a religion of peace. We are supposed to be kind, and polite. Even though you're a Christian I am not supposed to harm you," I explained to him.

"Anyone you see who is not behaving in this way, is not acting how a Muslim should," I said.

"Are you peaceful?" he asked.

"Very peaceful," I said. Instantly, my right leg bumped into the steel ladder I was standing on. I thought it was Allah trying to get my attention for something I had just said. I realized that I may have said something in the wrong way. *Humm, I hope I wasn't being too self-righteous*, I thought. So, I quickly internalized a Dua (calling upon God), *Allah, I don't know if what I said was wrong. Please forgive me. Please help me speak to him in a way that he can understand.*

"I don't believe in Prophet Muhammad," he continued.

"Okay. You're allowed to have an opinion," I responded.

"That's right, but I don't think women should cover everything. That's too much," he said, then proceeded to bring up the topic of the Taliban oppressing women. As I explained to him why we dress modestly and cover our hair, he argued that we could still be modest without covering our hair. He had a rebuttal for everything. So did I.

I continued to fulfill customers' orders and tried to maintain my balance on the staircase, but I felt someone's eyes were still on me. Our conversation continued as I picked items from the bins and placed them in the totes. He stood nearby to collect the totes once I finished. Then, a message appeared on the screen from my manager, instructing me to sign out of the system. Other associates on that floor were also asked to do the same.

The conversation continued.

"We love Jesus (peace be upon him). As a Muslim I have to believe in Jesus (peace be upon him) and all the other Prophets," I clarified.

"Really?" He asked with a surprised look on his face.

"We love and respect Jesus (peace be upon him), we just don't worship Him because we don't believe God is a human being. We see him as a Prophet," I told him.

"I still have more questions," he said. "What if I wanted to marry you? For example," he asked.

Is this guy trying to hit on me or learn about Islam? I questioned his intentions in my mind. If he was, he didn't stand a chance, but at least he was going to walk away knowing a little bit more about Islam.

"Are you married?" he followed up with another question.

Feeling like he was trying to get into my private life, I responded with an honest, "No," and proceeded to answer his question. "It's recommended for us to marry a Muslim man because there's more alignment that way. It's easier to understand each other and we wouldn't be having disagreements like the ones we are having right now, and the children would be raised that way."

He nodded, and the conversation continued.

"Even me being on the phone earlier, I'm not supposed to do that as a Muslim," I said to point back at my moment of weakness.

"It's not a big deal," he replied.

"I know, but as a Muslim everything matters. When you're at work, if you're not supposed to be on the phone, you shouldn't. You should be focused. Otherwise, that would be considered stealing," I said. "Islam is perfect, but humans are imperfect," I added.

After talking for an hour, it seemed he had so many more questions, but the shift ended. My goal wasn't to convert him. My goal was to help him see Muslims through a different lens.

"At the end of the day, God made us all. You're my brother. And we're Black," I said as I took my right hand and tapped my left hand to show him that, on the surface, we're the same even though our faith differs. "I appreciate you for asking all those questions. I'd rather someone try to find out why I am the way I am and believe what I believe than to just judge me," I said.

We had been talking for so long, other associates were looking at us. It made me a bit uncomfortable because I didn't want anyone thinking that I was a hijabi being hit on. As we both clocked out, I told him to write down his questions and I would try to answer them to the best of my ability the next time I saw him at the warehouse.

As I drove home, I replayed our conversation in my head. It felt like I had just gotten out of taking an exam I hadn't prepared for but ended up scoring high (I hoped). The questions had been blunt, and some comments made me uncomfortable, but I appreciated them because I knew that if these were his thoughts, other non-Muslims could have similar ones. But he'd had the courage to ask.

CHAPTER 7

Acts of Kindness from Non-Muslims

Despite living in a society that is filled with Islamophobia, there are still some kind and open-minded individuals. I took a break and went into the restroom of the first Amazon warehouse I worked at. As I made wudu (the cleansing process Muslims undergo before praying), there was a safety girl standing next to me washing her hands. Noticing how uncomfortable it was when I lifted my leg up to wash my feet in the sink one after another, she looked at me with raised eyebrows.

The safety girl wanted to know if this was habitual. We are not supposed to speak in bathrooms, but I didn't want to miss the opportunity of answering her question. She informed me that she was going to provide a way to facilitate the process for me and other Muslim associates. This comforted me, knowing that a Caucasian, non-Muslim was concerned about my safety as I engaged in a ritual different from what she was familiar with.

There was also a prayer room in this Amazon facility. The walk, like the first Amazon warehouse I worked at, felt like traversing the Great Wall of China. By the time I reached the prayer area, my feet were so sore I could barely lift them off the ground.

If I had to walk this much a few times a day to get to the prayer room, I would quickly run out of energy and would be questioned by managers about why I'd been away from my station for a lengthy period. I ordered a portable prayer mat from Amazon so I could at least pray in the break room.

One act of kindness I will never forget was when a non-Muslim covered for me while I fulfilled Sallah (prayer). Orders were coming in non-stop, but I had to stop because it was time to pray. While I prayed, a water-spider (an associate in charge of transporting and organizing totes in the warehouse) stopped what she was doing and picked out orders in my place so I would not fall drastically behind. She performed the task with speed and efficiency as she would for herself. In that moment, I realized that the biggest act of kindness a non-Muslim can do for a Muslim is to treat her like a human being and not stand in her way of worshiping Allah.

Later that same year, I parked my car near my house and quickly went in. In the morning, as I headed to work, I pressed the unlock button on the key fob but it would not unlock. Looking through the windshield, I could see that I forgot to turn off the headlights, which throughout the night had drained the battery. Almost in tears, I held the car keys in my hands and reflected on what minor sin I must have unknowingly committed to deserve this misfortune early in the morning.

I desperately looked to the corner of the fob to find the manual backup key, but the manual backup key, which was as slim as a corn-beef can opener, had disappeared.

Where did it go? Till this day I don't know. I stood beside the car and kept looking through the windshield, wondering how I could let the car die on me and having to call AAA roadside assistance twice in a year.

The sun rose, my shift began, but I was still hoping for a miracle. So long to my full day's worth of pay. A man with a Caribbean accent slowly drove by me. "That's your car? I noticed that the lights were on last night." He got out his car and offered to assist me. The only problem was, I couldn't even get in the car to open the hood.

He informed me that he was on his way to work but that I could use his jumper and leave it somewhere he could see it once I finished. That way, after work he'd pick it up. I had on the hijab, which meant that if he was aware of Islamic practices, he knew I was Muslim. He could have driven past me and thought to himself, *Just another serial killer covered in hijab,* but he didn't. Without even knowing me, he took a moment out his day to help me because I was a human needing assistance. That warmed my heart.

At the end of the shift, as all employees rushed down the stairs, if I were behind a male, he would open the door, and although he was in a hurry to go home, he would stand for a few seconds to hold the door for me. This did not happen with only one man. It would be a different man (Caucasian, Hispanic) on a different day. At that moment, they didn't look at me as a Muslim, they treated me like a woman. Another time, as I arrived at work, a Caucasian woman (an associate like myself) stood there for a few seconds and opened the door so I could enter. This blew my mind.

In the hallways by the staircases, non-Muslims would greet me. Whenever I took off to pray, I would remind the PA (Process Assistant) on that floor that I was going to pray in case he or she wondered why I was inactive in the system. One PA, once told me, "Take as long as you need to." Of course, I wasn't going to take forever to pray, but it was the most empathetic statement I heard from a non-Muslim.

To maintain the hijab in the West, I constantly must be my own hype woman. Before leaving the house, I remind myself of how stunning I look in my hijab. So, when

I don't get compliments from the outside world, I don't suffer an attention deficit.

One afternoon in my neighborhood, a girl, who I believe was not Muslim and was not modestly dressed, told me that I looked beautiful as she walked past me. "Thank you," I responded with a smile.

She may have thought it was just a compliment, but to a hijabi, that weighed tons. On different occasions, many non-Muslims have told me that I was beautiful in my hijab, which gave me more encouragement to keep it on. In a world that is so judgmental toward Muslims, still there were non-Muslims who regarded me as a human being with extra layers of clothes.

In the new warehouse I had been relocated to, the exterior and interior were embellished with creative artistry. It was always colorful and cheerful. It showed how much effort Amazon put in to ensure that its reputation of being an innovative brand transcended everywhere.

I walked in the Amazon facility during the Month of Ramadan and it felt like a surprise welcoming. As I entered and hurried to the timeclock to punch in, I couldn't help but to gaze at the decorations. The gold lettered balloons spelled Ramadan and the moon. The amount of effort the Amazon staff put in to bring awareness to a Muslim holiday made me respect the company even more. I felt welcomed even as I embraced my Islamic identity. Had I gotten hired at another company, who knew what type of discrimination or emotional distress I would have faced. That feeling of acceptance at Amazon made me realize how much Allah had looked out for my mental health and safety.

Though being at a warehouse was the last place I envisioned working at, as a new hijabi, this was a safe space for me, both emotionally and physically. But Allah Subhanahu wa Ta'ala had known it all along, because He is knower of the future.

CHAPTER 8
Prayer in the Workplace

Amazon operated strictly on metrics. Since I began working at the second Amazon facility I was transferred to, I had tried getting accommodation for my prayer time to be excused but was never given an answer nor a solution. So, I took matters into my own hands. Within a span of days, I had begun praying out in the open instead of inside the prayer room.

I had been assigned to a station on the first floor. I had already cleansed myself before it was time to pray. After picking out customers' orders for some time, I paused, laid my thin prayer mat on the floor, and fulfilled prayer. A Process Assistant from

Africa came behind me as I prayed and shielded my prayer area with the yellow totes that were stacked beside me.

As I prayed, footsteps were going back and forth behind me. Once I finished prayer, the African PA walked over to me and informed me that an associate had signaled to management that there was someone in the station without shoes on. I was shocked. Amazon's "if you see something, say something" culture was in full effect.

The PA brought to my attention a safety rule Amazon put in place that I had completely forgotten about—associates must keep their safety shoes on when they were in a workstation. Because I usually removed my shoes during prayer, I could no longer pray in proximity to my workstation. My thoughts began to race. If I could no longer pray in my workstation, did I have to go back again to the usual long walk to the prayer room? Luckily, he too was a Muslim. He explained he sometimes prayed in the break room (which was adjacent to the restroom).

Whenever I had to pray, I walked to the closest breakroom to my station. On one of those days, I got to the break area, but there were other PAs there. Part of me wanted to leave them there and walk to the prayer room, but I stayed because remaining saved me time.

"Hi, do you mind if I pray here?" I asked the PAs.

"Do you need us to leave?"

"No, no, you're fine," I responded.

They remained seated at a nearby table as I prayed. As someone who always valued image and how I would be perceived, praying publicly in a non-Muslim country helped me crush that fear.

Working at the second Amazon warehouse felt like an ankle monitor clutched on an offender; my every move was labor tracked. Once I signed into my station, every action and inaction were timed. There were moments when my manager called me over to figure out why I had a few gaps. "Oh, I went to pray," I would admit.

It was important for me to be productive and do my job as expected, but I needed them to also know that as a Muslim, when the Athan (call to prayer) goes off, I must make myself available to fulfil prayer. I had to explain to my manager that the sooner I prayed, the more blessings I'd get. And being punctual is better than prolonging my prayer and fulfilling missed prayers at home.

Explaining to my co-workers the importance of praying at specific times was like a sign language interpreter trying to communicate to someone who does not know the sign language alphabet. But somehow, someway, they got the message and respected it.

They told me that I had to clock out and clock back in every time I needed to pray. But that meant that the gaps would be deducted from my UPT (Unpaid Time). Knowing that I needed to pray more than once during my shift, in no time I would be left with no PTO (Paid Time Off) or UPT to cover my prayer breaks. Which meant that I would be fired.

I brought the issue up to my manager. With this problem in my mind, I was always next to my manager, either handing him an Islamic prayer schedule I downloaded from the site Islamic Finder or pleading for him to help me find a solution. After hearing from me repeatedly, my manager took a walk with me to Human Resources.

"There are other Muslims working here, but we don't have this issue with them," my manager said as he tried to resolve the issue.

"Every Muslim in America has this issue at work but not everyone speaks up," I responded.

More than one HR representative came together to get my situation resolved. Still, they could not figure out a way for me to pray without my UPT being deducted. The case was taken to upper management. I was told to go back to work, and they'd get back to me about a response.

In the meantime, I prayed and hoped that Allah would help me get this issue resolved so I could keep praying and still be employed. Within the same day, they got back to me! My UPT would no longer be deducted whenever I went to pray. I only had to let my manager know every time I was going to pray.

I remembered that Sallah (prayer) is the first thing that Allah Subhanahu wa Ta'ala would question me about. I could not imagine myself procrastinating prayer every day over a job. I'd rather be called that annoying girl who was always complaining about her UPT being deducted than missing an opportunity to earn blessings from Allah Subhanahu wa Ta'ala. In the end, I got to keep my job and fulfill my religious obligations because I showed them that prayer in the workplace was a part of my lifestyle.

CHAPTER 9
The Fall of the Twin Towers

In 1999, My mother and I were accorded a visa to visit New York for the first time, and one of my uncles took us to the World Trade Center. Upon arriving, we took the elevator and made a stop at the shopping centers. My mother recalls me being hyped to be there. "If it weren't late, we could have gone to the top of the building. You'd be able to see all of New York from there," my uncle said to my mother in my native language after he bought me a Tweety Bird backpack. My only memory from the World Trade Center was that Tweety Bird backpack. It was my first time and only time entering the World Trade Center.

Two years later, on the day the twin towers were attacked, I was in my neighborhood in Conakry, wandering around and daydreaming about my mother's return. At the time, Mama was pregnant with my little brother and stayed in New York. On September 11th, my mother had an eleven-o-clock appointment a few blocks from the World Trade Centers.

Since she still had some time to spare before her eleven-o-clock appointment, she decided to go to her ESL (English as a Second Language) class at eight-o-clock. When she reached the classroom, all lights were off. Which was unusual.

"We don't have class today?" my mother asked.

"We do. Just sit down and listen to the radio," her professor who was Greek responded.

"I think there's something going on at the World Trade Center," one of the students said.

The professor stepped outside for a few moments and then returned. "The second building was hit. This must be a terrorist attack," she said with her voice crumbling.

As the students rushed out, my mother suggested that her professor goes with her to her home since the professor's was far away. They walked four long blocks before arriving where my mother lodged at the time.

My mother's professor's husband worked at the World Trade Center. That morning, as he got up to prepare for work, his stomach began growling. His stomach-ache stopped for a moment, but as soon as he headed for the door to leave, his stomach began to feel upset again. That went on and off until he finally decided to go to the pharmacy to get medication that would calm his stomach down.

As he stepped outside the pharmacy, he noticed some smoke coming from one of the World Trade Center buildings. "That's my office!" he shouted. He ran into the elevator and got off where his office was. Upon arriving, he grabbed all the papers he could from his desk while screaming, "Fire! Fire in the building. Get out!" He kept alerting people. They were amongst the first to get out before the World Trade Center collapsed. Afterward, he was able to safely reunite with his wife, my mother's ESL professor. And my mother was able to travel back to Guinea after giving birth a few months later.

It did not occur to me how much 911 affected Americans until I migrated to the United States and was enrolled in school. My high school lectures were interrupted with fire drills. Even if we were almost through with a project or solving a problem, when the fire drill went off, everyone had to stop and look for an exit. We only returned when directed to. This left everyone restless and in a constant state of fearing for our security.

I wondered at times what life would have been like had I lost my mother on September 11th, since she was supposed to be right next to the World Trade Center. During the time I worked at the hair salon, I serviced a client whose mother worked at the World Trade Centers. My client, a mixed young woman, non-Muslim, whom I also went to the same college with, lost her mother during the horrific attack.

I did not wear the hijab at the time, but she knew I was Muslim. We bonded in a natural way. As I hovered over my client to style her hair, she held out a photo of her mother. I could feel the sorrow of an adult who longed to see, converse, and smell the scent of her mother one more time. I imagined what it was like spending her entire childhood without her mother by her side. I knew that no words could soothe her or bring her mother back. "I'm so sorry you went through that," I told her.

A month into my role at the second Amazon warehouse I was transferred to, early in the morning, the manager gathered Amazonians in a circle before the start of the shift. I had the impression she was going to give a speech related to the job. Instead, she grabbed a microphone and began talking about how 911 affected many lives.

I could feel a load of eyeballs looking directly at me, the only one there with a hijab on. If there were Muslim men present in that crowd, I could not tell because a beard alone does not reveal whether a man is Muslim or not, unless he had on a thobe and/or kufi hat. Many Christian men wore beards, too. But as a hijabi, my religious belief was always on display. It's as though I was being blamed for a terrorist attack that took place when I was nowhere near the crime scene.

Everyone heals at a different pace. Telling Americans to just get over the fall of the World Trade Centers is being insensitive. But for non-Muslims to blame every Muslim they come across for the fault of airplane hijackers is also incentive.

Over the years, the conspiracy theories I have heard surrounding the 911 attack are unending. The blaming, pointing fingers, hateful stares, and degrading will not erase what took place on that day. The trauma must not be brushed under a rug, either. It must be leveled to the forefront. Coming together, grieving together, must be encouraged, because the fall of the Twin Towers left a scar on the entire world.

CHAPTER 10

It's Not that I Don't Like You

I always found it exhilarating being surrounded by people who are different from me. Some of my closest friends have been people of a different race, ethnicity, and/or religion. In my high school days, we hung out, ate, and traveled together, had sleepovers, and exchanged personal stories.

Even though at the time I didn't look Muslim or fulfill all my religious obligations, deep down I knew that allowing my faith to dissolve in the presence of non-Muslims was a disservice to Allah Subhanahu wa Ta'ala. So, when it came to being involved in actions that associated partners with Allah Subhanahu wa Ta'ala, I had to exclude myself, because that was where the line had to be drawn.

When I was a teenager, a young Christian man bluntly told me that if I converted to Christianity, he would marry me. As much as I desired marriage, I knew that we would never experience our hair going gray together and racing with canes to the park.

During my days as a non-hijabi living in New York City—I don't know if on my forehead it said that I was spiritually lost—but I was always a target to Christian missionaries. In train stations, busses, the ferry, and on streets I would always be approached with a flyer and a "Jesus loves you" statement. I would give a listen for a few moments, accept the flyer so they didn't follow me the entire day, and then walk away in a hurry. Though at the time I was not doing much to become a better Muslim, my heart was attached to monotheism.

One day, I had just concluded an event where I was a guest speaker, and two Christian women (one who I'd known for a few years and the other I had met that day) and I joyfully conversed. As we were about to part ways, they invited me to join them for church. "I have to go home," I told them. They went their way, and I went mine.

Had we stood there and conversed more, I would have attempted to let them know that me turning down their invitation to church did not signify that I had something against them or disliked them. "It's not that I don't like you. It's not that I don't like Jesus (peace be upon him). It's not that I am not open-minded. I just don't want to displease Allah," I would have told them.

Christmas is the most wonderful time of the year for Christians. But as a Muslim living in the West, it's a time when I must figure out a way to say "I don't celebrate Christmas" without sounding rude.

"Merry Christmas!" one of the process assistants at Amazon greeted me as I entered our department. Without responding, I headed toward my station. Thankfully, the sound of the totes passing through the conveyor belt was so loud that my silence was unnoticeable.

"Next," the post office lady behind the thick glass said. I walked up and slid my package under the counter. Just when it was time to pay, I realized that I had left my debit card in the car. As I was preparing to leave, she blurted, "Merry Christmas!" with a smile on her face. I responded with silence. Her smile turned into a slight frown. Quickly I stormed out of the post office.

That same day, when I got home, I ran into my Hispanic neighbor. "Merry Christmas!" she said.

This time I felt the need to say more. "I don't celebrate Christmas, but God bless you," I told her.

I was wearing the hijab at the time when these four interactions unfolded (the invitation to church, the PA at Amazon, the post office lady, and my neighbor). I assumed that because I started wearing the hijab, non-Muslims would understand that I belong to a different faith. I thought that the veil on my head clearly expressed Tawheed (the belief that there is only one God who is worthy of worship). But apparently it did not.

This taught me that many non-Muslims are surrounded by Muslims and have yet to find out what Islam stands for. We live in the same environment, yet the lack of awareness is apparent. That there are still some who perceive Muslims as unapproachable beasts whose identity is associated with the Taliban, ISIS, Boko Haram, and anything barbaric.

However, they did not know that the essence of Islam is peace and the belief that there is only one God and He alone is worthy of worship. I felt unseen and misunderstood.

The young man who wanted to convert me for marriage, the two ladies who invited me to Church for prayer, the PA at Amazon, the post office lady, and my neighbor were all nice people. Their intention may have been to let me see what they perceive as beautiful about their faith. But I could not take part in it because they were inviting me toward something that is completely against my belief (Shirk). Worshiping anything or anyone other than Allah Subhanahu wa Ta'ala is Shirk. It is the most severe, most grandiose, most egregious sin, an insult to Allah (the one and only Creator of the Heavens and Earth, mankind, animals, the seen and unseen). So, when I had to choose between pleasing them and pleasing Allah, I had to choose Allah.

Excluding myself from actions that displease Allah was not only pertaining to when non-Muslims attempted to lure me to commit Shirk. When my family or Muslim friends invited me to participate in activities that were deemed non-Islamic, I avoided it because I did not want to be in an environment that made me reminisce my past.

My natural disposition was to be a people pleaser. I got a kick out of making others happy, even if sometimes that dug me in a hole. Saying "no" meant risking being called mean, boring, selfish, or anti-social. And who wants to be labeled that?

I had spent so many years of my life saying "yes" when I should have been saying "no." Had I continued to be this way, I could have never been a better practicing Muslim, because to be a Muslim means having the courage to say "no" when what I am asked to do goes against what Allah Subhanahu wa Ta'ala demands of me.

Rectifying my relationship with Allah made me more self-conscious. When I found myself avoiding certain gatherings, it was not that I didn't like the person or people. It had more to do with the fear of hindering my relationship with God. Again.

CHAPTER 11
Stages of Modesty

Stage 1. Fear

So many thoughts hovered over me as I prepared to put on the hijab. I wondered if I would be able to keep up with the standards it entailed. A family member told me that it would be harder to find another husband because my beauty would be covered. And that it would be harder to get a good job. I wanted to remarry at some point in my life. I wanted a better job. But I knew those whispers were trying to discourage me, and no matter how much I wanted a husband and a better job, I was going to stick with my plan.

Stage 2. Relearning

There was so much that I didn't know about Islam. Each time I listened to Islamic lectures it became more apparent to me that there was a myriad of information I missed out on over the years and needed to tap into. I stopped chasing people and started getting to know the word of Allah Subhanahu wa Ta'ala.

The Qur'an is written in Arabic because that is the language the Lord of the worlds—Allah Subhanahu wa Ta'ala—chose to reveal the message in. The Qur'an is Allah speaking to mankind, as it was sent down by the Angel Jibril (Gabriel) and revealed through Prophet Muhammad (peace be upon him) over a span of twenty-three years.

Because I wasn't fluent in Arabic, I purchased a Qur'an that was translated to English. Being able to understand English made it easy for me to wrap my head around the message my Creator intended for me to learn.

Although I was born into Islam, growing up I did not put in the effort to learn about Islam. Hence, in my adulthood I had to relearn Islam to become a better practicing Muslim. There is a myriad of Islamic scholars who teach the message of Allah Subhanahu wa Ta'ala. However, in the beginning of my learning stage, choosing "the right" (which is subjective) scholars for me had a big impact on my spiritual journey.

For me, it was not only about hearing the message but more so about how the message was delivered. I related more with Islamic scholars who had a sense of humor, were straight forward, passionate, and gentle. And if some of them had a tough approach, I received the message without feeling attacked or defensive. I just needed to hear the truth.

Some of the scholars focused more on Fiqh (Islamic law) and others focused on Duas (supplications) that Prophet Muhammad (peace be upon him) made. They made Islam sound exciting, which motivated me to keep learning and bettering myself. As I listened to my favorite scholars, the more I wanted to open the Qur'an.

Stage 3. Reflecting on the Whys

For so long I was judging Islam based on how others behaved and their opinions about Islam. Humans are flawed, but the word of Allah—the Qur'an—is perfect. I was no longer going to wait for someone to give me diluted answers. Once I sought out information for myself, it became easier to submit to God's will.

Extensions

Not only is it prohibited for Muslims to have extensions in their hair during prayer, but it is also an act which Allah Subhanahu wa Ta'ala wants the believers to stay a from to appreciate the way He created them. Extensions had been a part of my life since childhood, to the point where it had become difficult to break free from it as an adult. Since I had a deep desire to have hair that gave me an exotic look (long and voluminous), I frequently got microbraids, box braids, and weaves.

I got so hooked onto extensions that even when I needed to make a quick run to the grocery store that was only a block or two blocks away from my house, if I didn't have extensions in my hair that day, I would wrap my natural hair with a scarf before heading out. In those moments, I didn't cover my hair out of obedience to Allah but rather out of insecurity. I was tricking my mind by telling myself that the reason I put different types of extensions in my hair was to explore and be spontaneous with my look. But what did my addiction to extensions imprint in my subconscious for all those years? That I was not enough.

Over the years, my sensitive skin could no longer cope. Slowly, I noticed that when I put extensions in my hair, especially synthetic, I would have an allergic reaction. White patches would appear around my edges and neck. I didn't need a dermatologist to point out to me the cause of my skin being irritated. Even though extensions had become noticeably unhealthy for me, I kept putting them in because I was not completely pleased with the length and texture of my natural hair.

Not only did I start putting extensions in my hair in Guinea around the age of eight, but I also allowed a neighbor in our Bronx apartment to perm my hair when I was ten years old. The irony is that, in my twenties, when I stopped putting extensions and chemicals in my hair, my natural hair grew beautifully. It may never reach the floor, but it became healthy and grew to a length I deemed reasonable.

As a hairdresser, I dealt with all types of hair. Hair that was so long knots were formed as I braided. And in some instances, it was like needing spiderwebs to connect edges. Don't get me wrong; all hair is beautiful. The problem wasn't that clients' hair was long or short. The problem was that no one was satisfied with what God gave them.

When the Kardashians got two French braids, there was a spike in French braid requests at the salon I worked at. Mostly Caucasian and Hispanic women flooded our salon trying to mimic the reality stars. They would ask to add extensions to their already long hair. "You really don't need fake hair," I would tell my clients who naturally had long hair. The tip was good, but my remark went in one ear and got out the other.

Growing up, I and many Black women and men around me had the impression that ALL Caucasians, Asians, and Hispanics had hair that grew past their bra strap. However, as a hairdresser I was exposed to reality. When a Caucasian, Hispanic, or Asian woman walked in our salon asking for her extensions to be taken out, we the hairdressers—who were mostly African— would look at each other in disbelief. As if to say, "that's not her real hair?"

In a society that is superficial, I felt like I could never reach the beauty standard promoted on TV. It is innate for a woman to desire being noticed, and women put an incredible amount of effort to look presentable when stepping outside of the home. So much so that some walk around with the air blowing through their locks as if it is their natural hair, when it is not.

Once a woman steps outside of her home or comes across photos of other women on the Internet or television, she can begin to compare the length and/or texture of her hair to that of another woman. Also, men compare what they see outside, on the Internet, and TV to that of the women in their lives (wife, mother, sister, aunt, etc.).

What happens when the woman being compared to puts extensions in her hair?

This leads to women and men having beauty expectations rooted on falsehood. That is why Allah Subhanahu wa Ta'ala wants women to appreciate their natural hair and not give off the wrong impression of perfection. When a girl or woman covers her hair and body, others have less room to judge her or compare themselves to her. Which is one of the reasons it is important for her to practice hijab.

Allah Subhanahu wa Ta'ala created every living thing with wisdom. If He wanted all women to have hair extending to their waist, He could have done so. But He didn't. Different hair length is part of God's plan for each person/race to be distinguished. Attempting to forcefully have something that my Creator did not intend for me meant that I was displeased with His decree. I had to figure out a way to do away with my insecurities and accept myself the way I was created.

Hijab

It is clear to me! Females are a weakness for males. Countless times, I've gotten a kick out of watching how men behave when they see a woman. When a female walks by wearing clothes that reveal her shape, it does not matter her age or what her face looks, I've seen many uncles, husbands, and fathers turn their heads to look at her, or look from the corner of their eyes. When I see a male and then a female, I instantly have a betting game going on in my mind because I always guarantee myself that the male will look. And I always won the bet.

An Ah-ha moment for me was when one day, as I was heading to work, I walked behind a man, and in front of him was a curvy woman wearing leggings that left nothing to the imagination. As she took each step, everything jiggled. It was as if she was walking around with no underwear to keep her goodies sheltered.

I was wearing hijab, but the way that man eyed her up and down made me feel like he was undressing me with his eyes. *I feel sorry for guys. So that's why Allah ordered women not to wear clothing that is tight and see-through in public,* I thought to myself. It seemed like that man was willing to request VTO (Voluntary Time Off) from work just to look at that woman's derrière. It made me reflect on how many heads I made turn and hearts I disturbed when I used to wear attire that was revealing.

Moments like this motivate me to be cautious about what I wear in public, because although in the Qur'an Allah Subhanahu wa Ta'ala first instructed men to lower their gazes and guard their chastity and then for women to do the same, if I wear something that is revealing, it becomes even harder for men to fight their reflex. We are created beautifully, so of course we are a weakness for males.

Before wearing the hijab, when I heard from Muslim men that a woman must wear the hijab, I would roll my eyes, assuming that it was man's attempt to suppress a woman. I also heard Muslim women who didn't wear the hijab say that wearing the hijab was a choice, and I believed them. Why? Because I didn't read the Qur'an to truly understand the word of God, and it was a way for me to take the easier route. But when I finally read the Qur'an with an open mind, I understood that wearing the hijab was indeed a choice. It was a choice to either obey or disobey God's command upon women.

As a young woman, often I heard non-hijabi young women in my community say, "When I get married, I'll wear the hijab for my husband." I noticed a trend where women started wearing the hijab as soon as they married. So, I thought the main reason for wearing hijab was to submit to a man's ego and appear as an obedient wife.

But later, through reading the Qur'an and listening to lectures by Islamic scholars, I concluded that it is the contrary. The hijab is worn for Allah Subhanahu wa Ta'ala, but because of the female's decision to submit to God's command, she is not objectified in society, and the husband reaps the benefits (i.e., he has a tranquil heart knowing that other men are not lusting after his wife).

To wear the hijab properly, I had to refrain from relying on diluted information about hijab or looking at how other hijabis wore the hijab. I did my own research to familiarize myself with the dos and don'ts of hijab so I could practice them to the best of my ability.

The hijab is not just about dressing modestly. It is about taking precautions and putting a barrier between myself and anything that could have a negative impact on my spirituality. Hence, I must be selective about what my eyes look at, what my ears listen to, what my hands touch, where my feet go, what I put inside of my mouth (e.g., Halal food, non-alcoholic beverages), and what comes out of my mouth (e.g., abstain from cursing, lying, backbiting, flirting, vulgar speech).

Polygamy

In my ignorant days, without fully knowing the history of Islam, I went as far as to assume that the Qur'an was written by man to benefit man because of its support of polygamy. Hence, for many years I had doubts about Islam and was not motivated to learn more about my faith.

Polygamy was the missing puzzle piece I needed to find to complete my sincere belief in Islam. When I did find that one Islamic scholar on YouTube who clarified it for me, I felt a huge burden fall off my chest. It made me trust Allah's wisdom even further. Getting the answer as to why polygamy is allowed in Islam is an integral part of my spiritual journey.

As I gained the trust of my co-workers at the first Amazon warehouse I worked at, a curious, Caucasian young man asked me, "How come Muslim men can have four wives?" Had he asked me that prior to me knowing the answer, I would have been irritated. Instead, his question came at a time when my doubts had dissolved, and I was happy to give him an explanation.

Throughout my life, I heard some men in my community say, "if you want to fix up your wife's act, get a second wife!" These men found themselves practicing polygamy out of ego, only to end up regretting their decision later. Instances like this defeat the purpose of polygamy and tarnish the image Islam.

Prophet Muhammad (peace be upon him) had wives from different tribes after his first wife (a widow) Khadija bint Khuwaylid (may Allah be pleased with her) passed. All his wives were witnesses to his great character. He never had secret wives. When he did practice polygamy after losing his first love, it was out of purpose, not ego, or only for the sake of fulfilling lustful desires. He married widows, divorcees—women whose circumstance was not appealing to a potential candidate. Since he had wives that were previously married, he also took care of children that were not his own. He treated them all fairly.

Prophet Muhammad (peace be upon him) married only one woman (Aisha bint Abu Bakr, may Allah be pleased with her) who had never been intimate with another man. Yet he fulfilled the rights of all his other wives, even though some of them were widows and divorcees. This showed other men that women deserve to be under the protection of marriage. As the last Prophet of Allah, he was chosen to be an example to mankind. In the manner that he dealt with his wives, this served as an example to men who would come to marry virgins, divorcees, and widows.

Fornication and adultery (major sins) are highly disliked and forbidden by Allah Subhanahu wa Ta'la. The Creator has laid down a solution for every problem mankind may encounter. With the population of women exceeding that of men, Allah Subhanahu wa Ta'ala made polygamy permissible so that women could have the opportunity to be taken care of. In turn, this allows both men and women to fulfill their lustful desires under a covenant and have the stability marriage can offer.

Some men's sexual desires are so heightened that one woman is not enough for them. Instead of stepping outside of their marriage and committing adultery, Allah Subhanahu wa Ta'ala made it permissible for him to marry another woman, but only if he can respect the conditions laid out: treat his wives fairly/equally, provide for them, and protect them.

Allah Subhanahu wa Ta'ala made it an obligation for men to be the protectors and maintainers of women. If a man comes across a woman he finds attractive, he cannot just use her for a one-night stand because he is having marital problems, impregnate her, and run off to another town or country. He must first marry that woman and fulfill her rights. As I explained polygamy to the curious, Caucasian young man at Amazon, he nodded. Though he was Christian, he walked away with a better understanding of why Muslim men can have up to four wives.

Prophet Muhammad (peace be upon him) was married to one woman (Khadi-

ja bint Khuwaylid, may
with her) for twenty-five y
to practice polygamy after he
shows that monogamy is pract
lam. Listening to the many reaso
some men in my culture chose to pra
polygamy, they made it seem like marry
four wives is an obligation a Muslim man
must fulfill, and one that a Muslim woman
can't escape. Whereas Allah Subhanahu wa
Ta'ala made polygamy an option, depend-
ing on the circumstance.

As I dug deep and learned more about
Islam and listened to the explanations
of religious leaders whom I admired and
respected, the less skeptical I became. I
learned more about our beloved Prophet
Muhammad (peace be upon him), the reasons why he had many wives, and the way
he was gentle with them—which was opposite of what I had witnessed in the Muslim community and stories I heard growing up.

Knowing that polygamy is not permissible in Islam only so that men could exert
their masculine power over women and be
intimate with more than one woman made
me see that a woman is honored in Islam.

Allah be pleased
ears. He began
r death. This
iced in Is-
ns why
ctice
g

and pushed

e four wives
and that he
emotional,
han a man
ie side he
n and day
n a closet
ie garage,
t his bank
account having a negative balance.

Prior to understanding polygamy, I had the tendency of looking down on women who were in a polygamous marriage. Since having a clearer outlook on polygamy, instead of looking down on women who are in polygamous marriages, I've come to respect them for being able to handle it.

I have spoken to first wives who expressed to me that they had no problem accepting their husbands to marry another wife. It takes immense selflessness for a woman to put aside her jealous tendencies and put up with seeing the man she shares everything with have another wife so that other woman can also experience companionship and her rights being fulfilled within a covenant. I believe that every woman wants to be the only woman. But some women have the heart to cope with polygamy without going bananas. Though my desire is and has always been to be in a monogamous marriage, I am pleased to know that I follow a religion that encourages selflessness.

Stage 4. Acceptance

Every time I stand before a mirror, I am utterly shocked! Why? Because I cannot believe that of all people, I am wearing the hijab. It feels like I am looking at a different person, someone who has gone through different phases in life and has come to accept that doing what pleases God brings contentment. I can barely look at myself in the mirror without thinking of my past.

You know what else the mirror reminds me?

Growth.

Stage 5. Maintaining My Personality

I knew that if I were to fully embrace the hijab, I needed to keep a part of me—my personality. The hijab didn't stop me from being the outgoing and goal-driven person that I am. I didn't suddenly push my goals onto the back burner, sit home, and do nothing.

Instead, the hijab made me embrace my religion, become more self-aware, and set boundaries that would protect me from disobeying Allah Subhanahu wa Ta'ala frequently. I was enthused that I could embrace my religion, continue being myself, but adjust some areas of my lifestyle to become a better practicing Muslim.

I didn't want to give others the impression that I have become stiff and unapproachable because of the hijab, because by nature I am very playful. But I also have my serious side. Of course, now that I wear the hijab, I am more careful in how I interact with the opposite gender because I don't want my giggles to be mistaken for being flirtatious and my presence to make men with the wrong intentions think they could shoot their shot. But when surrounded by women, I am a lot more relaxed, and I want to continue being the person they can laugh, connect, and converse with about anything.

Being stubborn in a healthy way is what makes me unshakeable when it comes to what I firmly believe in. And I pray that Allah Subhanahu wa Ta'ala keeps it that way for me. I only wish to move forward in my spiritual journey. Therefore, I constantly ask Allah Subhanahu wa Ta'ala to keep beautifying the hijab for me. I never want to assume that the devil can't come to me and influence me to think that I made the wrong choice by wearing hijab.

Stage 6. Introspection

Before the hijab, I had the impression that I was AMAZING. Living in a society that constantly reminded me to exceedingly toot my own horn didn't help matters either. The hijab brought me back down to earth and made me notice the bad qualities/habits (according to Islamic standards) I had that hindered my spiritual growth.

The more I noticed my list of imperfections, the more I was inclined to seek knowledge to better myself. As much as I was aware of the parts of me that were good, I had to hold myself accountable for the parts of me that were not so appealing and needed improvement.

I had been disobeying Allah Subhanahu wa Ta'ala for over twenty years. I spent
two decades of my life running through a
maze, and then I finally ran into an open
door of redemption, which led to others of
unending Islamic knowledge I needed to
absorb. Within just a year's time, He guided my heart to wear the hijab, embrace an
Islamic lifestyle, and made me aware of the
bad qualities/habits I needed to work on.

Once I began wearing the hijab, I realized that there were parts of my personality that I gave up over the years just to
assimilate into the Western culture. I realized that I am very comfortable with
covering my chest, legs, etc. because I am
naturally a private person. Over the years
as a non-hijabi, I sometimes found myself
wearing revealing outfits that displayed
my bust and legs not because I liked to do
so but because I saw other women doing it.

Not only was I uncomfortable, but I por-
trayed an image that deep down was not
me. Men wowing and women admiring my
figure made my head bigger, but my soul
was empty. Wearing the hijab made me feel
like I was in my safe space again. Although
I am outgoing, I am protective of my space

when I need to. The hijab did that for me. Like I could have full control over who gets to look at my body parts. The hijab holds me accountable of remaining true to what I value.

For many years, I chased after people, sought to be accepted and loved. When I didn't receive the acceptance I craved, I felt like I wasn't good enough. Wearing the hijab gave me the ultimate confidence booster. If I could put on a head cloth that turns people off or makes me hated by so many and still have a smile on my face, then surely I don't need to be liked by everyone, nor do I need to try to be a people pleaser in every situation.

With the hijab on, I felt like if the entire world decided to ignore me, I'd be okay, because I have Allah Subhanahu wa Ta'ala. Having this renewed mindset was what allowed me to not seek validation, be too clingy, to turn down invitations, or say "no" when someone crossed my boundaries. It made me look forward to sitting in my corner and bask in "me time." It made me become comfortable with being a loner in moments I needed to.

Stage 7. Islamic Greetings and Expressions

Although I was born a Muslim, I did not grow up with the habit of using Islamic greetings at home or outside of the house. I got so accustomed to not using Islamic greetings in the presence of Muslims that when I started wearing the hijab it was as though I was being judged even more for not doing so. Training my tongue to say "Assalamualaykum" (peace be upon you) and "Jazakallah Khair" (may Allah reward you with good) felt like learning my ABCs all over again.

When it became slightly easier for me to say the Islamic greetings and I greeted Muslims who were not used to me greeting them that way, they did not greet me back the Islamic way. "Look at her, she thinks she's righteous now," I would imagine was their impression of me was. Deep down I knew I wasn't trying to act righteous. I was practicing ways to please Allah. But moments like these made me want to retreat into a shell.

Stage 8. Comparison

Part of what made it easy for me to embrace the hijab was that I made a conscious decision to stay away from things that could affect my Iman (Faith) and clung on to the word of God. When I unfollowed celebrities that I subconsciously idolized over the years, I began to regain my individuality.

Although wearing the hijab was by far my biggest milestone, it came with some challenges. Since within a short period I was religiously achieving things that were harder for others to do, a part of me thought that I needed to slow down. For example, I had decided that I was going to wear a full hijab and not show my neck publicly.

By the grace of Allah Subhanahu wa Ta'ala, this was very easy for me to do. But when I saw that there was a trend where hijabis sometimes styled their hijabs in a way that revealed their necks, I too, one day, posted a video in my Instagram story where I had my hair covered but my neck showed.

However, I realized that I was on my own journey and needed to stop trying to fit in, even in the hijabi crowd. In no way was I above or better than them, but their weaknesses weren't mine. Instead, I had to stop comparing my journey to that of others, laser focus on my personal weaknesses, and understand that I didn't have to slow myself down to match others' speed.

Stage 9. Nonjudgmental

As someone who for many years experienced life without the hijab, I understand the discomfort a non-hijabi might feel when a hijab-wearing woman gives her a judgmental look.

As I was on the bus one day heading back home from the hospital, a beautiful young lady boarded the bus with a crop top that showed off her belly piercing. I was wearing hijab. I looked at her once and instantly looked away because had I stared too long, she would probably feel like I was judging her.

Once I started wearing the hijab and taking it seriously, naturally I felt uncomfortable whenever I noticed someone dressing immodestly or acting in a way that was outlandish. But I always remind myself that a person can only act according to her level of understanding. And I was once there. No number of judgmental stares or complaints could have made me practice hijab.

I wore the hijab when Allah guided my heart and made me understand the importance of it. In situations where a hijabi wears the hijab improperly, I often say to myself, *May Allah forgive us.* Why didn't I think to myself *May Allah forgive her?* Because I don't want to instill in my mind that I am superior or more righteous than her. I know that my hijab may not always meet Allah's standards, either. Having this understanding allows me to treat all women the same, whether they are dressed modestly or immodestly.

Stage 10. Shame and Regret

As a perfectionist, I wanted every aspect of my life to be error-free, but it turned out otherwise. When I crossed over to a more God-conscious lifestyle, looking back at my spiritual journey made me feel shame and regretful. At the back of my mind the should've, would've, could've slowly crept in to haunt me.

However, knowing that the devil's whispers are meaningless and distracting, and Allah Subhanahu wa Ta'ala is the Most Merciful and loves Tawbah (returning to Allah by repenting and changing one's ways), gave me comfort and hope. Whenever these thoughts crept in, I used them as motivation to strive even harder to prove myself to my Creator.

The perfectionist in me wondered, *Why did it take me all those years? How come my parents didn't teach me more about my religion?* They spent all their energy and money investing in my secular education, but not as much on my religion, my Hereafter. I had to carry the heavy load of frustration, and forgive my parents and myself for not knowing better.

Instead of viewing myself as the child who got left behind on religious affairs, I vowed that I would take over the wheel and influence the trajectory of my spiritual life. I would work on becoming a better Muslim for myself and so that one day I could assist my children as they travel through their spiritual journey.

Despite feeling shame and regret, I accepted that if my parents had never invested in my secular education, most likely I would not have become a writer. And I've acquired so much beneficial knowledge about my religion as an adult. I believe that this is the best time for me to learn from my mistakes, because as an adolescent, the Internet or YouTube was not at my disposal.

The information settled better in my heart as an adult since I was able to browse through the Internet and listen to numerous lectures on YouTube at my own pace. Instead of playing the blame game, I accepted the fact that it was all part of Allah's decree for me to go through this journey. Allah's timing is the best timing, and He is All-Knowing.

Stage 11. Facing Petty/Uncomfortable Moments

During the COVID-19 (Coronavirus Disease 2019) pandemic, my family and I drove up to Philadelphia for a two-day getaway. As we arrived, the usually populated resort was silent and empty because of the pandemic.

That evening, I headed down to the indoor swimming pool. There was practically no one there, but one family. As I dipped my foot in the pool to test the temperature of the water, children looked at me and then at their parents. Again, they looked at me and then at their parents. It was as if they wanted their parents to give them an explanation as to why I was fully covered in the pool. This was my first-time swimming in public as a hijabi, hence I had on modest swimwear which covered my entire body except my face, hands, and feet.

A few moments passed by. I could tell that they still wanted to swim, but my presence made them uncomfortable. How did I know that? They got out of the pool I was swimming in (which was indoors) and walked over to the outdoor pool that was separated with glass doors. I watched them as they played around and joyfully swam on the other side. They took social distancing to a whole other level. Either they never swam in the same pool as a colored person, my swim gear creeped them out, they were afraid of catching COVID, or all three. I was offended, but on the bright side, I had the entire pool and jacuzzi to myself.

My hijab did not only affect how others viewed me. Those who found themselves around me also were judged. One morning, I drove my mother to work and parked a distance from where she was supposed to get out. Somehow, as I pulled out into the driveway, they saw me covered in hijab. They were non-Muslims. My mother told me that the next day, she was told not to show up there anymore. It rubbed me the wrong way that my mother went through that because she was seen around me. But life had to go on, and my hijab had to stay on.

Muslims are taught to aim to be the bigger person when a situation arises; to choose peace over quarrelling. Though I am a woman, Black, and Muslim—all three can make me an easy target to pick on—I don't want people to think that they could pick on me and get away with it. I know when to speak up and stand my ground when I feel violated, and other times I allow things to slide to prevent the situation from escalating.

Another time, my mother's car was due for inspection. As I pulled to the sideroad and parallel parked, I noticed two guys to my right standing by a tree with a smirk on their faces. With my hijab on, they could see that I'm Muslim. On the car in front of me was an empty, recyclable plastic cup, a straw in between, and the yellow McDonald's logo displayed on the exterior. Someone had finished drinking it and left it on the car's roof.

I went into the house for some time. When I came back out, in front of me was that same empty, recyclable plastic cup. Instead, this time someone had deliberately taken it from the other car's roof and placed it on the car that I drove. I looked around, and the two men with the smirks were no longer there. For a flashing moment, a part of my conscience told me to stick around and confront them, the other part of me told me to "relax, it's not worth it." I grabbed the empty cup and drove off. During petty moments like these, I become slightly amused knowing that had it not been for my religion being my moral compass, I would have acted out of character just to prove a point.

On the day Mother's Day was celebrated in the United States, I had taken on an extra shift. Just another busy day at Amazon. As I made my way to my station, a middle-aged Black man who looked like he spent day and night at the gym, greeted me. I greeted him back.

After a few minutes he asked, "Do you have kids?"

"Not yet," I responded.

"Oh okay. I was going to wish you happy Mother's Day," he said.

I turned toward the pod and continued working. A few minutes passed by, and I lifted my hand to reach for the scanner and noticed that it was missing. In front of me, the man who had greeted me earlier had a scanner that he wasn't using at that moment.

"Can I use your scanner?" I asked.

He didn't give me his. However, he pointed toward the station behind me just a few steps away. I walked over to another station where no one was working, grabbed the Handheld scanner, and walked back to my station.

"From the way you're walking, you're about to have kids soon," the man said.

I quickly looked away from him, trying to avoid responding to his vulgar comment that made me feel uncomfortable.

Shortly after, "Are you married?" he asked.

"Engaged," I said.

"Muslim men can have four wives, right?" he asked.

"Not my husband!" I responded. We both chuckled. "They can have four wives, but they don't have to. And he can't just marry another wife without speaking to his first wife about it," I told him.

The man looked surprised at the latter comment.

"It takes a righteous woman to accept it. A selfless woman," I explained.

"I've never heard it from the woman's perspective," he said.

I nodded and continued working. Had I snapped back instantly the moment he spewed a vulgar comment, I most likely would not have had the opportunity to clarify some misconceptions he had about Islam.

Four months later, when I landed at John F. Kennedy Airport, I encountered another scenario. When my flight landed around seven p.m., I remembered that there was a course that I had signed up for on that day. By seven-thirty p.m., I logged into Zoom to take part even though I was stuck in a never-ending line that led up to security.

Once I claimed my baggage and got through security, I hurried out to secure a cab. The heavy smell of nicotine and the sound of pompous police sirens greeted me first. Travelers scattered everywhere as each looked for a ride back home. I searched for a private cab service, but every cab that pulled over was already reserved.

I stood outside and waited for my course to end. When the course on Zoom finally ended at nine p.m., I searched for a private cab service, only to find out from someone that I couldn't get a private cab there. He directed me to where I could at least get a yellow cab. I went back in the airport, where travelers waited in a Nile River shaped line to take a cab that the airport dispatched.

After waiting in line for roughly ten minutes, it was finally my turn. I was looking forward to finally sitting back in a car, relaxing, and fantasizing about what I'd eat once I got home. The dispatcher told me that I could get in whatever yellow cab that was available next. The person in front me had already gotten in a cab, which meant that any cab after her should provide service to me.

I grabbed my two pieces of luggage and two handbags, and walked up to the next available yellow cab. Right before I could reach the car, the driver briskly swerved past me. Noticeably, he had no passengers. I moved up a few steps again to get in the next available yellow cab, and that driver also swerved past me. Clearly, he also didn't have any clients.

I didn't exchange a word with those two drivers that avoided me. They didn't know how far I was going, nor did I ask them for a discount. I wasn't with children that looked like they'd drool all over the car or scratch the back of the driver's seat like a cat. So, what was their excuse for not servicing me?

Within seconds, my brain processed it was because I was Muslim! I swallowed my frustration and kept pulling my luggage. The following yellow cab pulled up. Without me saying anything, an Indian-looking man who appeared to be in his fifties or sixties stepped out of the driver's seat, grabbed my baggage, and placed them in the trunk.

I thanked him, took a deep breath, said Bismillah (in the name of Allah), and sat in the back of the car. As the cab pulled out of the airport, we conversed. He seemed easy-going, so I bombarded him with questions of how profit is split with the airport. I was moved by his motivation to work six days a week, over twelve hours daily, to provide for his family.

Five to ten minutes into our drive, "Where are you from?" I asked.

"Bangladesh," he responded.

"Oh! I have a few friends from Bangladesh," I said.

"Where are you from?"

"Guinea," I responded

"That's in...?" he asked.

"West Africa," I said. "Are you Muslim?" I asked.

"Yes!" he responded cheerfully.

"MashaAllah," I said, smiling as I looked through the window to my right.

Two drivers avoided me because my hijab revealed I was Muslim. The third driver, a Muslim, saw my hijab and was willing to service me. The discrimination I experienced at JFK airport was a glimpse into the ramifications of Islamophobia in a society, because to be a hijabi in the West means being marginalized without having uttered a word.

A month later, as I stood in a public area and browsed my phone, I couldn't help but look at myself in the glass door that was in front of me. It showed me a reflection of what I wore that day: black and pink Reebok protective shoes, navy blue sweats that almost fit like leggings, and a black Trench Coat that reached four inches above my knees.

Hmmm, these sweats are looking too tight on me, I pondered. And, before I could even finish my self-critiquing thoughts, someone said, "Excuse me? Can I ask you a question?"

I looked up and a few inches to my right stood a slim, tall, Hispanic-looking man.

"Yes," I answered underneath my Coronavirus mask.

With the mask covering my mouth and the hijab covering my head, ears, sideburns, and neck, the only thing uncovered were my eyes. I looked directly at him but tried not to stare too hard.

"Nothing. I knew you were beautiful. I could tell just by looking at you from the corner," he said while eyeing me up and down.

I couldn't believe that for a second I thought he'd called me because he wanted directions.

Yup, this must be a confirmation I'm not wearing hijab properly, I thought to myself.

This pick-up line sounded way too familiar, and I figured he had been saying that to any woman who passed by. I knew the next thing he'd try to ask for would be my number. So, before he could even say "can I," I opened the glass door that weighed more than me, left him hanging, and rushed toward the bus stop.

"Yo! Yo! Yo!" I heard him holler; the echo of his voice escalating as I moved away from him, one big step at a time.

Welcome to New York City, where even if you're trying to be modest some men want something from you.

Stage 12. Understanding God's Power and Mercy

Throughout my life, even when I wasn't practicing Islam the way I was supposed to, Allah Subhanahu wa Ta'ala still blessed me in ways that I didn't deserve. All around me, from mother nature to the occurrences that even science could not justify, I had a firm belief that there's ABSOLUTELY a higher power that's in charge of everything. Reminding myself that He has the power to give and take away what's been granted to me within a blink of an eye pushed my focus on prioritizing my relationship with Him.

Allah Subhanahu wa Ta'ala is also the Most Merciful. Even if I spent most of my life not being my best self, if when I have an epiphany and decide to do better, He can turn my mountain of sins into a mountain of good deeds. There's light at the end of the tunnel if I choose to amend my ways. That gives me hope to do better.

Stage 13. Failing Forward

Mankind's greatest enemy is the devil. Although the hijab has empowered me to be less of a people pleaser now, the devil has a way of creeping in. As the saying goes, "If the devil can't get to you directly, he'll go through the people closest to you to get to you." When it comes to me, there are things I've vowed to stay away from. Since the devil can't talk me into doing certain things anymore, he goes through my family.

There are moments when my mind is made up about not being a people pleaser, then out of nowhere, a situation arises where if I don't agree or accept, a family member will be dissatisfied, and I find myself once again saying "yes" when a "no" would have been satisfactory to God. When I do feel like I've slipped and fell back on my people pleasing ways, ignoring the wrath that Allah Subhanahu wa Ta'ala could have, I repent and try to do better next time.

If I'm going to fail, I choose to fail forward. I choose to always crawl back to Allah Subhanahu wa Ta'ala because I know that even though I have the intention of pleasing my Creator a hundred percent of the time, sometimes I may fall short because I'm human.

Stage 14. The Reward

Every day is a challenge choosing between what I want to wear and what Allah wants me to wear. What I want to say versus what

Allah prefers I say. How I behave or how Allah wants me to behave.

To identify as a Muslim, I must wholeheartedly believe that there is a Hereafter. Which means that Allah Subhanahu wa Ta'ala will question and hold me accountable for every word I utter, and action taken while I'm alive. Whether I am in Guinea or New York, Allah is watching me. Whether my status on Facebook shows online or offline, Allah is watching me.

Why not post a thirty-second video on Instagram of me challenging Cardi-B to a dance off and become an International Bestselling Author within seconds? Why remain modest in a country that does not require modesty? Why choose modesty when being modest disqualifies me from certain professional opportunities? The reward.

Many don't see the point of keeping covered a body that is beautifully created when it is steaming hot outside. Nor do they understand the point of making oneself uncomfortable to please the Creator of that body. However, just as the main motivator for working long hours at a job is a salary, the motivator for keeping the hijab on is the reward that is promised.

The reward of the sacrifice made to please Allah Subhanahu wa Ta'ala can be seen and felt first in this life. Second in the Hereafter. When Allah rewards, He has no limits. In this life, the reward can come in the form of ease for some. Others may not find ease in this world because of their decision to wear the hijab, especially if they live in an environment that brutally and openly oppresses Muslims. For such people, the reward will come later or in the Hereafter.

As for me, I feel my reward in this life, and hope that when I meet with Allah Subhanahu wa Ta'ala He will reward me in ways I can't imagine. When I decided to wear the hijab, I saw many doors open for me. Doors that many told me would be shut because of my hijab.

Prior to committing to hijab, I had a list of things that I asked from my Creator, but how much was I willing to sacrifice to follow his obligations upon me? The doors of blessed sustenance, peace of mind, increased beneficial knowledge, clarity, hon-

or, and a healthy marriage opened for me when I chose to sacrifice for my Creator. By doing that which He loves, Allah—the independent deity in control of every aspect of my life—gave abundance.

In school, the surest ways a student can become a teacher's pet is by maintaining good grades and behaving in a way that pleases the teacher. Other classmates may mock and label the teacher's pet as a geek for spending nights in discomfort with their nose in a book studying, but in the end, the teacher's pet gains a favorable position. I don't mind being mocked in this world for embracing hijab. I would rather have the last laugh in the Hereafter.

When Allah Subhanahu wa Ta'ala has declared an act (i.e., wearing hijab) mandatory, anyone—rich or poor, short or tall, light-skinned or dark-skinned, literate or illiterate, he who fulfills that becomes someone who He loves. I chose the reward over comfort because I wanted to be amongst the people who Allah loves.

CHAPTER 12

The Truthful Scale

Deciding to wear the hijab full-time while residing in the United States was a 360-degree change for me. It was one of the toughest decisions I had to make but one that came with great reward and gave me peace of mind. A few people told me that if I wore the hijab, my life would go backward. But instead, what I witnessed was blocks of blessings layered upon more blocks of blessings cemented by Allah Subhanahu wa Ta'ala and sent my way.

Looks fade, but the beauty of the heart remains when it is cleansed continuously. Why waste my energy seeking attention from men when there is always going to be someone who looks better? Instead, I can take that energy and work inward. That is what Allah Subhanahu wa Ta'ala values most.

My spirituality was at the far end of the spectrum, and now I prioritize inching closer to God. In my journey of spiritual growth, I internalized that life is not about showing off everything I've been bestowed and making heads turn. It is about being centered with who God wants me to be and owning it. It is not about me knit-picking on how others (Muslims and non-Muslims) choose to live their lives. It has more to do with me being sincerely satisfied with my Islamic identity and knowing that to be adequate, I don't have to be a chameleon in the West with the rest.

Allah Subhanahu wa Ta'ala, with His infinite mercy and patience, beckoned me toward a God-conscious path even though I neglected Him for years. This is not a declaration that I've reached perfection, nor will I ever reach that level, because I am human.

Like committing to anything in life, wearing the hijab is a responsibility. God gave humankind the privilege of choice. He understands that in choosing, I may opt for a different route than the one He wants me to follow, because I am imperfect. However, that is why He extends His mercy and will forgive and redirect. Over and over, until the palpating heart stops and the soul is taken.

I did not haphazardly fall out of the sky and land on earth to live an undisciplined life. No matter where I stand in my spiritual journey, I am still worthy of growth and getting closer to my Creator. The distorted image the media portrays about Islam is far from how I experience Islam. Islam pushes me to hold myself accountable for the way my actions affect my relationship with my Creator, myself, and others (Muslims and non-Muslims).

Wearing the hijab has been quite a journey for me and will continue to be a journey until the day I return to God. My hijab journey is not only about me becoming more modest, but it is also about rediscovering myself through Islam. I am more than a woman covered by a cloth; my personality adds a different sauce to a world that is a melting pot.

No amount of people-pleasing or social media fame could exempt me from facing the scale of truth on the Day of Reckoning. I've lived through tides and tried to right my wrongs, but despite making wrong turns on earth, on the Day of Judgement when I face Allah Subhanahu wa Ta'ala, when my deeds are weighed on the truthful scale and I await my eternal sentencing for the Hereafter, I can tell my Creator, "Allah, I have tried."

Printed by Amazon Italia Logistica S.r.l.
Torrazza Piemonte (TO), Italy